JAMES T. DRAPER JR.
TRUSTING THY WORD

BROADMAN PRESS
Nashville, Tennessee

© Copyright 1989 • Broadman Press
All rights reserved
4212-90
ISBN: 0-8054-1290-5
Dewey Decimal Classification: 248.4
Subject Heading: CHRISTIAN LIFE
Library of Congress Catalog Number: 88-35600
Printed in the United States of America

Library of Congress Cataloging-in-Publication Data

Draper, James T.
    Trusting thy word / James T. Draper, Jr.
        p. cm.
    ISBN 0-8054-1290-5
    1. Bible. O.T. Psalms CXIX—Criticism, interpretation, etc.
2. Word of God (Theology)—Biblical teaching. I. Title.
BS1450 119th.D73 1989
223'.207—dc19   88-35600
                                                    CIP

Trusting Thy Word

Dedication

To Bailey Stone
my friend and God's instrument
in confirming my call to preach God's Word

Contents

1

The Key to a Happy Life

Psalm 119:1-8

I. **HAPPINESS IS PRESERVATION FROM DEFILEMENT:**
vv. 1-4

    1. From Defilement of Our Hearts: v. 2*b*
    2. From Defilement of Our Habits: v. 2*a*,3
        (a) God's Word Teaches Us the Way of God: vv. 3*b*-4
        (b) God's Word Teaches Us the Will of God: v. 2*b*

II. **HAPPINESS IS PRAYING WITH DIRECTION:** vv. 5-6

    1. The Shame of Sin: v. 6
    2. The Strength of Surrender: v. 5

III. **HAPPINESS IS PRAISING WITHOUT DEFILEMENT:**
vv. 7-8

    1. Cleanness: v. 7*a*
    2. Correctness: v. 7*b*
    3. Conduct: v. 8*a*
    4. Confidence: v. 8*b*

Psalm 119 is the longest of all the psalms. In fact, with 176 verses, it is the longest chapter in the Bible. It is particularly related to the Word of God. Nearly every verse, all but five for sure and some claim only one, contains a synonym for the Word of God.

The Word of God in verse 1 (or stanza), for instance, is called "the law of the Lord." In verse 2 it is called "His testimonies," verse 3, "His ways," verse 4, "Thy precepts," verse 5, "Thy statutes," and so forth. This is the case in all 176 verses of Psalm 119. So, it is a psalm about Scripture, about the Bible.

It has a most intriguing arrangement. Over verse 1, it says "Aleph." Over verse 9, "Beth," verse 17, "Gimel," and the like. Those are letters in the Hebrew alphabet. Each of these sections in Psalm 119 has a different letter of that alphabet. It is significant because every verse in the section begins with the Hebrew letter of the alphabet which heads that section—a beautiful poetic device. It is one of the most cherished, beloved psalms in all of the Book of Psalms.

The settings and times of Psalm 119 were similar to our own day. It was a time of rampant religious skepticism. Verse 126 singles out that religious skepticism. It was a time of sickening apathy, indifference, and fickleness. The people changed quickly. Their attention span was short. They jumped from one fad to another. Verse 113 bears this out. We discover in verse 95 that it was an era when the people of society were thoroughly profane. It was a wicked, gross period.

The psalmist is a young man in that kind of hostile environment, one hostile to faith and to the things of God. He finds himself the object of derision, slander, and opposition, and he is having a hard time handling it. He is struggling with life and the opposition of a hostile society around him. But when confronted with that hostility, it simply causes him to tighten his grip on the Word of God. He doesn't turn loose of it—he grabs hold of it. He shows us how we should respond to opposition and hostility. There is a blessedness that comes from reading the Word of God. This psalm points this out, and this first section begins with two "blesseds" which are beatitudes.

"Blessed are the undefiled in the way, who walk in the law of the Lord. Blessed are they that keep his testimonies, and that seek him with the whole heart" (vv. 1-2). There is a special joy and blessedness from reading, learning, and keeping the teachings of the Word of God. This sounds similar to Revelation 1:3 where it promises blessedness to those who read the words of the prophecy of Revelation and those who hear it and take it to heart. That is a synopsis of what is promised here in Psalm 119. Blessedness and happiness come when we read and appropriate the truths of the Word of God into our lives.

God wants us to be happy (joyful in Paul's sense), and He gives us an approach that works. It is not theoretical or philosophical. It works and is practical in our lives. What God wants us to understand is: He is the only one who can fill the emptiness of the human heart, which longs for fulfillment and happiness, and God is the only one who can give those to us. These verses lead us to that truth.

Happiness is preservation from defilement (v. 1). Undefiled means those who are "kept from evil." Aren't we glad God delivers us from sin? It doesn't matter what sin it is. God delivers and frees from all sorts of evil. The church of Jesus Christ stands as a living testimony that God delivers us from our sins. What we have in this first section of Psalm 119 is the flip side of that.

Happiness is not only being *delivered from* sin, it is being *preserved from* sin. God wants to preserve us from sin. The world yells, "Do what feels good." Whatever you do, it will not bring satisfaction. It will provide a momentary thrill, but then the sinner will want "more, more, more." There is within us an insatiable hunger that cannot be satisfied by the defilements of the world. It doesn't matter what it is. It is a proven fact. One starts smoking marijuana, and it leads to cocaine, heroin, and you name it. You start flirting with immorality—then you engage in it. Then there may be perverted expressions of sexual license. And the sinner wonders why he is never happy. He is unhappy because evil and defilement cannot usher in happiness. *Happiness is being preserved from defilement.*

It expresses itself in two ways. *First, we are preserved from defilement of our hearts.* Sin and defilement start in the heart. We never do an evil act without preconditioning to do it. In our hearts sin is conceived. Jesus declared in Mark 7 that evil comes from within, on the inside. "Seek him with the whole heart" (v. 2) means an *undivided* heart. It implies that we give Him our undivided attention. Some have had difficulty finding God in their lives. Perhaps they have been too casual about it. They go their way, "do their own thing," disregard God, and casually, almost sarcastically, deal with God.

To find the peace of God in our hearts, we must turn our whole attention to God. We are first preserved from evil in our hearts. "Ye shall seek me, and find me, when ye shall search for me with all your heart" (Jer. 29:13). There is a preservation from the defilement of the heart. In the Word of God we discover cleansing for our hearts. We are to memorize Scripture. Thereby we are preserved from the defilement of our hearts. There, waiting for us is truth and a message for our hearts. We love the Word of God because we recognize the Word of God as the sayings of God for our hearts. We don't worship the Bible. We worship the God whom the Bible declares. We know of God because of His revelation in His Word.

Second, we are preserved from the defilement of our habits. What is in our hearts we will do. "Who walk in the law of the Lord" indicates an action, a habit of life. ". . . That keep his testimonies" again implies a habit of life. ". . . That seek him," "they also do no iniquity: they walk in his ways," are all indications that if we believe the right thing in our heart, if we know the Lord there, we will be preserved from defilement in our life-style.

This passage teaches that when we come to God for direction of our habits and of our conduct, we discover two truths. *First, we discover the way of God.* The "way of God" is that we live in a manner that is consistent with Him. God is a Deity of holiness and purity. We become aware of the kind of life that a holy, pure God wants us to live.

"Way" in the Hebrew always refers to a path, a road, a highway, a thoroughfare you would travel to reach a destination. The picture here is that we move in the way that God is going and walk in His ways with his character. "Way" could refer to the character of God. We must walk in a way consistent with His character. "This is the way, walk ye in it" (Isa. 30:21). Isaiah speaks concerning the joy of ultimate redemption and calls God's way "the highway of holiness" (Isa. 35:8). There is happiness in holiness. *The Word of God preserves us from the defilement of our habits by showing us the way of God.*

The Word of God also teaches us the will of God. The will of God means God's purpose. We can discover what God's design for our lives is. It is amazing that God has a will for every person's life. He cares about our lives and has a plan for us. He is interested in what concerns us. The Word of God preserves us from the defilement of our habits by leading us to discover the will of God for our lives.

"Law" in verse 1 is the word "Torah." "Torah" literally means "that which is given out," "that which is taught." So when we speak of "walking in the law" it means all that God has taught. It consistently refers to all of the Scripture. Some people use the expression, "we are not under law but under grace," to rationalize their behavior. It is true we are not under the Levitical Law, but we are to walk in the Law, the Torah, all that God has taught us. Torah appears over twenty-five times in Psalm 119. We discover in the Word of God that we are preserved from the defilement of our habits by obeying God. Happiness comes to those who treasure the testimony of God, discover the will of God, and live according to that will.

Happiness is praying with direction (vv. 5-6). To ascertain the essence of praying, we must pray under the direction of God. We are to pray so that God's Spirit guides us in our praying. The psalmist is not talking about praying casually or flippantly. In this context, it means praying consistently with the Word of God.

Beginning at verse 4 is a prayer. The psalmist is not preaching anymore. He is praying. He prays with direction, and in verses 5 and 6 are two elements praying with direction involves. *He prays with the direction of the Word of God which is the shame of his sin (v. 6).* "Then shall I not be ashamed" (v. 6). When is "then"? When he keeps His commandments. When he obeys God and lives according to what God wants him to be, then he will not be ashamed. He will have respect for all of God's commandments.

When we pray with direction, we first of all pray with the consciousness of the shame of our sin. God's Word is a mirror in our lives. It reflects oneself. When the Word of God reveals to us an inconsistency, a rebellion, a sin in our lives, we are to confess it to Him. We are to repent. The Word of God brings conviction, correction, and constructive instruction. The severest judgment the Word of God speaks of is to people who know to do certain things and fail to do them. Many have no shame over their sin. Many prayers are hindered because we are unwilling to consider the commands of Christ. Sin is rationalized and excused. Sometimes we take Scripture out of context and justify our sin by trying to make it "biblical."

The worst tragedy in America is that we have lost our sense of shame. We are no longer ashamed or embarrassed. We kill 1½ million babies a year and have no shame over it. We have allowed pornography, because of our hesitancy and cowardice in taking a stand in our communities, to become a multibillion-dollar business, and it degrades all it touches. It destroys a society. People live in open adultery and brag about their degradation. We put it on the front pages of our newspapers, and if that weren't sensational enough, we have scandal sheets that distort the truth. We have no shame—many enjoy reading that kind of trash. We cannot pray with direction without having a shame for our sin. We ought to be so embarrassed before God.

The psalmist has so meditated on the Word of God he is moved by the blessedness of being preserved from defilement. Then he is stirred to be obedient to the Word of God and longs for it to become a habit in his life. He is conscious of his weakness, and his longing becomes a prayer to God. He views his sin and realizes that only through God's power can he possibly obey and be what God wants him to be. He prays in a sense of the shame of his sin.

Praying with direction also involves the strength of surrender. "O that my ways were directed to keep thy statutes!" (v. 5). One of the ways we pray with direction and decisiveness is that we have surrendered our lives to God. We must come humbly before the Lord with a surrender to God's will. No wonder Proverbs 28:13 says, "He who conceals his sin does not prosper but whoever confesses and renounces them finds mercy." We find strength when we obey God. If we want the strength of God in our lives, then we must be obedient to Him. We must surrender to the will of God. Happiness in praying with direction, with a sense of shame of our sin, and with the strength of surrender.

Happiness is praising without defilement. From prayer to praise is never a long journey. Spurgeon observed, "Be sure that he who prays for holiness will one day praise for happiness." We praise without defilement. For the psalmist, his shame has vanished; his silence has been broken. Now there is praise. The essence of praise is adoration of the person of God. It is a life focused on God, and it is praise without defilement. "I will praise thee with uprightness of heart, when I shall have learned thy righteous judgments. I will keep thy statutes: O forsake me not utterly" (vv. 7-8).

You cannot praise God with a tainted life. Unless your heart is pure, you are not praising God. He does not accept praise that is based on a sinful life. Neither does He accept an individual that comes without confession of sin. That is why many people are not happy coming to church. They don't "get anything out of it." That speaks volumes about their relationship with God. You must confess your sin. It doesn't mean you are perfect. None of us is perfect, and we don't have to become perfect before we can come to church. Yet, the only way to be truly happy is to have such a cleansed life that we can praise Him without defilement. God is serious about holiness and purity. It is important for us to approach Him as He tells us to, and we approach him, first of all, with confession, repentance, and surrender. Then we can praise Him without defilement!

There are four things with which the psalmist praises God.

First, he praises Him with cleanness: "I will praise thee with uprightness of heart . . ." (v. 7). A pure life honors and glorifies God. It glorifies God to bear His character. His character is purity. *Second, he praises Him with correctness:* ". . . When I shall have learned thy righteous judgments" (v. 7). Praise is learned from the Bible. In fact, when we study the Bible we are praising God. When we open the Word of God, read it, and meditate on it, we are praising God. We praise God anytime we esteem His word as precious as He does. We could call our Sunday School hour "The Hour of Praise" because we are never praising God more than when we are studying Him. Plenty that is called "praise" today is mere human emotion, not praise correctly prescribed by the Word of God. Correct praise involves more of a concentration on the Word of God and allowing it to express itself through our lives.

Third, we are to praise Him with our conduct: "I will keep thy statutes" (v. 8). The praising life is one that obeys the Lord. We cannot really praise Him if we are not being obedient to Him. Jesus said, "If you love me, keep my commandments" (John 14:15). We praise Him with our obedient conduct.

Last, we praise Him with confidence: "O forsake me not utterly" (v. 8). We cannot keep these statutes unless God helps us, so the psalmist's cry is, "God, don't stop helping me." Isn't that what the Lord's Prayer is? "Lead us not into temptation." We praise God when we recognize and acknowledge our dependence on Him. The psalmist asks God not to forsake him utterly. No smug self-righteousness here. Not an arrogant man. He is praying, "Lord, I cannot do it without you. I want to obey you. Please don't forsake me." We must be dependent upon the Lord every day. We must not labor in the energy of the flesh. Nothing will wear us out quicker than trying to serve God in our own strength. When we serve in the power of the Holy Spirit, in the awareness of His presence in our lives, there is an exhilaration. When we truly praise God in Spirit-filled power, with all of our hearts, there is a release of strength. We then have divine resources and to depend on God is to praise Him. We praise Him by dependence on Him.

This portion of the psalm teaches that happiness is preservation from defilement of our hearts and habits. It is praying with direction, and as we do that, we will know by the Word of God the way of God and the will of God. As we pray like that, it will be with cleanness and correctness. We will pray in our conduct consistent with His will and with confidence as we depend on Him.

God wants us to be happy. He wants us to have fulfillment. This section of Psalm 119 reminds us that in discovering the heart of God and the will of God, doing what God has given us to do, we will have happiness, peace, and fulfillment in our obedience. The key to happiness lies in an understanding of His Word, His will, and His way for our lives.

2

How to Survive Adolescence

Psalm 119:9-16

I. **THIS QUESTION INVOLVES INSIGHT:**

  1. Memorizing Scripture: v. 11
  2. Maturity: v. 12*b*
  3. Meditation: v. 15

II. **THIS QUESTION INVOLVES IMPRESSIONS:**

  1. Let submission be your hero: v. 12*a*
  2. Let surrender be your happiness: v. 14
  3. Let sharing be your hobby: v. 13

III. **THIS QUESTION INVOLVES INTENTION:**

The first word of verse 9 is "how." That is the typical question of youth. *How.* As my children were growing up, their perpetual question was "how?"—a logical question which makes sense. It is not wrong to have honest questions. All through the Bible questions are asked.

For instance, in Deuteronomy 18 the nation of Israel asked, "How can we know when the message has not been spoken by the Lord?" That was a good question, wasn't it? Job asked, "How can man be righteous before God? How can one born of woman be pure?" Mary, the mother of our Lord, when informed that she was going to bear our Lord Jesus Christ, asked, "How will this be, since I am a virgin?" That was a good question too. "How" is a biblical question. We ought not to be afraid to ask "how?" When we come to this passage of Scripture, "How can a young man cleanse his way?" (v. 1). he is really asking, "How can young people survive adolescence? How do you make it through these years?" It is very difficult to do. How can one survive these youthful years?

Adolescence is a time of transition between childhood and adulthood, between dependence—where parents do most of the structuring—and interdependence. Notice I did not use the word *independence*. The dread tragedy today is that young people are growing to maturity thinking that the opposite of dependence is independence. The opposite of dependence is *interdependence*. We never come to the place where we do not need other people, where we never interact with others. We must remind ourselves that we don't go from dependence to independence. Adolescence is a period when we are moving through that season.

One reason adolescence is so tough is that the stages of adolescence do not occur chronologically. Neither do they necessarily occur exactly alike in every young person. Of course, every young person is different. God has provided variety in His creation. We cannot look at other adolescents and recognize how it is supposed to be. It doesn't happen logically. Rather, there are five critical areas through which we pass that change us and play significant roles in our lives.

The five critical stages of adolescence are:

1. Developing an independent identity. Young people are in the process of becoming individuals, of developing personalities that are distinct from their parents and from other people.

2. Interpersonal relationships. They are in the process of developing communication and social skills. They are learning to communicate without a sense of self-consciousness, becoming a part of a group.

3. Boy-and-girl relationships. We hear many casual remarks about this stage, but it is a serious phase of growing up, when boys and girls become sexually aware. They begin to relate to the opposite sex. Adults need to be sure they are setting a proper example for them in that relationship. These relationships cause stress and strain on adolescents.

4. Decision-making. They are learning how to make decisions and how to avoid making decisions merely because others make them. They face "peer pressure." They must find the courage to make decisions based on their own values, and they are discovering what their values and beliefs are.

5. Learning about God. Who is God? How relevant is God to my life? During the teen years, young people begin to have serious questions and doubts about Christianity. It is all right to do that, a normal part of going through adolescence.

There is nothing easy about going through adolescence. These five areas are dangerous. Adolescence is like a dark canyon with the bridge out. How are you going to pass through it and survive it? During that time many young people go through various stages of inferiority feelings, feeling dumb, hearing unkind nicknames, awkwardness, insecurity, hurt feelings, emotional highs and lows, and the like. All of these matters are real and serious. Add to that the fact that during adolescence teenagers' bodies are changing physically. The pituitary gland wakes up, and the hormones seem to be going crazy. Many don't know what to do with these drives and urges. Their emotions seem to be felt more keenly, more strongly during this time than ever before or after. That adds to the complication.

James Dobson notes that the primary reason for adolescent distress is that youngsters do not fully understand what is happening to them. (See his book *Preparing for Adolescence*).

In the midst of all this, the Word of God is realistic and practical. It does not have an ivory-tower complex. It is not removed from where we are. It looks at us exactly where we are, and it meets us where we are. It is a Source every age can approach to find direction for their lives. The psalmist was apparently a young person. He was asking the typical teenage question, How? "How can a young man survive all of this pressure?" It is an honest question, and God is big enough to handle any question, any doubt, any fear.

This question has a tough answer. ". . . by living according to God's word" (v. 1*b*). Now is the time for us to ask another how? "How do you live according to God's Word?" It is simple to decide that is what we are supposed to do, but how do we do it? How do we go from where we are to where we ought to be? These eight verses treat the three aspects of human personality that are absolutely critical for adolescence—indeed for all of us. They deal with the intellect, the emotions, and the will. Those are the three battlegrounds all of us face as we grow through the adolescent years and on to the end of our lives.

The psalmist is speaking concerning believers. The first prerequisite to making it through these years, or any years, is to turn from sin and receive Jesus Christ. This is a psalm written to believers who want to grow through the adolescent years and on to maturity wisely and successfully. They want to survive these rough years resoundingly.

How do we survive? *This question involves insight or intellect, and there are answers in the Word of God.* There are answers to our intellectual questions. This question How? is intellectual. When we turn to the Word of God, when we receive intellectually the truth of God, God gives us answers. In the Word of God there is the answer to every important question we could ever raise. The answer may not be in specific detail, but God confirms answers through His Word. He presents us enough of an answer that we can develop and turn it into trust and commitment. Following Christ is not a leap into the dark—it is a leap into light! If we follow what God declares in His word, we will not go through life leaping into the dark, jumping to conclusions. Rather, we will walk with confidence, "Stepping in the Light," as the old hymn goes.

The psalmist suggests that we can survive adolescence by three actions. *First of all, we ought to memorize Scripture.* "Thy word have I hid in mine heart, that I might not sin against thee" (v. 11).

Paul says, "Let the word of Christ dwell in you richly in all wisdom" (Col. 3:16, KJV). The Israelites were commanded to memorize Scripture: "Therefore shall ye lay up these my words in your heart and in your soul" (Deut. 11:18). We are to hide God's words in our hearts, not for concealment but for security. We memorize the Word of God and place it in our hearts. Therefore, it is always ready for instant and constant use to keep us from sinning. We are kept by the Word as we store the Word in our hearts. The best material is God's Word, the best place is my heart, and the best purpose is "that I might not sin against thee." To help us grow up and survive adolescence we must memorize the Word of God. It sharpens the intellect and sensitizes the heart to all challenges.

"Blessed art thou, O Lord: teach me thy statues" (v. 12). *The second step toward surviving adolescence is maturity or teachability.* We are called to be disciples, and a disciple is basically a student. We are learners. Man's teaching will make us more learned, but God's teaching will make us more holy. God's teaching will persuade us and enlighten us. Nothing is forced upon us. We need to be teachable.

When a young person is unteachable through adolescence, he/she grows into a rebellious, angry misfit. He is angry at the world. There is always a tension between himself and others. The reason is that God does not force maturity, it is taught, and we must be teachable, even though we may not understand some of what we hear. Life is like a journey. We plan to carry certain items with us when we take a trip. The same is true of life. However long one's life is, it is a long journey, and how foolish it would be not to pack what we need on that journey.

If we are going to survive adolescence intellectually, we must learn to meditate. "I will meditate in thy precepts, and have respect unto thy ways" (v. 15). We are to consider God's ways and Word. When we speak of meditation, it is not just contemplation. We memorize the Word of God, think about what He has spoken, and then we apply it. The Word of God is not simply information for our heads. It is inspiration for our hearts and lives, causing us to respond in a way that is healthy and wholesome. We survive adolescence by memorizing, by maturity, and by meditation.

This question also involves impressions, what we feel intuitively. This is an emotional question. How? How can I do this? Our emotions are perhaps felt more strongly during the adolescent years than at any other period, but we cannot trust our emotions. They are cyclical and unreliable. There is danger in acting on our impressions and living by our emotions. One's emotions have to be made accountable to his reason and to his will. Our emotions may not be right. A classic example of that is what pilots would call vertigo. Flying in a fog or in a cloud a pilot cannot use the horizon as a point of reference and, though the instruments may indicate which way he is going, his feelings may tell him something else. A pilot took off from Arlington (Texas) Airport a year or so ago in a dense fog. Within a matter of seconds, it crashed two miles south of the runway. The pilot had no point of reference and, though his instruments revealed what he was doing, his feelings told him he must turn the plane. When he did, he dived right into the ground. Oh, the unreliability of our feelings!

That is why when we become angry and write a hot letter, it is a good idea to sleep on it. Let your feelings have a chance to change before you take rash action. When we let our emotions speak instead of our intellect, we will usually have trouble. We never reach a time when we can trust our feelings. One of Satan's tricks is to cause us to respond emotionally, to rely on our feelings. He delights to stir our emotions and make us vulnerable. Most of the tragedies that occur, whether immorality, drugs, murder, child abuse, etc., come during moments of high emotional appeal and pitch. One's emotions need to be made accountable to one's mind and one's will—and that needs to be directed by the Word of God.

The psalmist teaches us how we can survive emotionally. There are two answers. *The first is submission.* Through this psalm he refers to the Lord. The Lord of the Old Testament is the Lord Jesus of the New Testament. If we want to survive emotionally the adolescent years, we must come to that moment when we submit to Jesus Christ as Lord and Master. We must reach the place where we want to please Him. We want to respond as Jesus would respond. We make Him Lord of our lives and our Model. One heartbreak today is that a large percentage of our youth have no role model, unless it is an actor or rock singer. They have no one they can look to with admiration. But we can look to Jesus with admiration.

Human heros, even religious heros, will all eventually fall. James 5:17, concerning Elijah, states he was a man of "like passions as we are." That means he is just like us. Think about Elijah for a moment. One minute he was on Mount Carmel calling God's fire upon the prophets of Baal. He was a national hero. Everyone was looking to Elijah with respect. A short time later he was running into the desert because he was afraid Jezebel was going to kill him. He was depressed, and he wanted to die. All heros, even religious heros, have feet of clay.

Jesus will never fail you. He is the same yesterday, today, and forever. He can be trusted. He will never lead us down a deadend street. If we want to survive emotionally in this topsy-turvy world, we must understand what it means to submit our lives to Jesus Christ.

The second answer is similar, but it involves a slightly different turn. *If we are to survive emotionally, we must learn the secret of surrender.* "I have rejoiced in the way of thy testimonies, as much as in all riches" (v. 14). Submission is the esteem with which we hold the Lord Jesus Christ. We submit ourselves to His Lordship. Surrender is the practical outgrowth of that submission— obedience to Him. Remember that Jesus asked, "Why do you call me Lord and don't do what I tell you to do?" To call Him Lord is to submit to Him, but the natural outgrowth is surrender, obedience. When we delight in the Word of God, we will want to do what He tells us to do.

Conversely, being obedient to the Lord means *there are some things we will not do*. If we will do what God requires of us and wait, God will give us the best. If we will obey Him and surrender our lives to His will, He has a marvelous plan. All we have to do is allow Him a chance. If we mess up our lives with disobedience and rebellion, He is unable to give us what He really wants us to have.

He has a perfect plan for our lives. Plan A is absolutely magnificent. Don't make God use plan B, plan C, and so forth. Wait for God's best and surrender to His plan. That means saying "no" to drugs and alcohol. Christian young people have no business tampering with drugs/alcohol of any form. The best reason for staying away from them is that God wants us to protect our bodies. Do not put into your body anything that robs your ability to be responsive to God. That is what narcotics do. They keep you from making wise decisions, from thinking straight. Alcohol and narcotics attack your spiritual life faster than anything else. Stay away from them. If you want to survive emotionally, surrender your life to the Lord.

A third answer to surviving emotionally is sharing. "With my lips have I declared all the judgments of thy mouth" (v. 13). The psalmist is verbalizing the truth that God has given to him. We need to be verbalizing our faith. If you want to be a strong, surviving teenager, maturing effectively and happily with satisfaction into adulthood, you must learn to share your faith in Jesus Christ.

This question "how" involves the intent or the will, the volitional quality of our lives. How will one survive adolescence intellectually, emotionally, volitionally? One can do it if he is anchored, solidly based upon Jesus Christ.

How many expressions of personal commitment there are in this passage! "I have sought thee" (v. 10). "I have hid thy word . . . that I might not sin against thee" (v. 11). "I have declared thy judgments" (v. 13). "I have rejoiced in the way of thy testimonies" (v. 15). "I will meditate in thy precepts" (v. 15). "I will have respect unto thy ways" (v. 15). "I will delight myself in thy statutes: I will not forget thy word" (v. 16). That is an extra-strong commitment.

Contrary to what many believe, we have the capacity to make a firm commitment of Christ. "How can I survive adolescence?" involves choices young people make. We have the capacity to make a commitment of our lives to Jesus Christ. Daniel was a teenager who survived victoriously, and the secret is found in Daniel 1:8: "Daniel purposed in his heart . . ." He made a resolute commitment in his heart.

Joseph, in Egypt as a slave boy, found Potiphar's wife sensuous, immoral, and desiring to compromise him. But Joseph had made a commitment to the Lord and would not compromise that commitment. Don't wait until you are in the arms of a lover to make moral decisions. You don't have to wait until you are in a potentially compromising situation to decide what you are going to do. Young people get into trouble morally because they act out of feelings and not responsibly. Making a responsible commitment to Christ will protect you.

How do you make the commitment? It is like crossing an intersection. If you are a good driver, you will think for the other fellow, as well as for yourself. Even if the light is green and you have the right-of-way, it is foolish not to look at what is coming. There are many intersections in the world where it doesn't really matter who is right. What matters is who is left! There is no consolation if you get killed, and you had the right-of-way. When you approach the intersection, you have certain choices to make. You can foolishly go ahead without any consideration of what might be approaching. If you do, chances are you could be hurt or even killed.

What will you do? Yield? Or decide, I want my way, and go on in dangerous territory? What will you do?

When God's will and your will intersect, you must choose; will you yield to the will of God or will you go on foolishly doing what you want?

Remember: commitment is yielding to the will of God.

3

How to Face Reality

Psalm 119:17-24

I. **EXAMINE OUR DEPENDENCE:** vv. 17-19

   1. Dependent for life itself: v. 17
   2. Dependent for insight into His Word: v. 18
   3. Dependent for guidance through life: v. 19

II. **EXPRESS OUR DESIRE:** vv. 20-21

   1. Motivated by recognition of humanity: v. 20
   2. Motivated by God's rebuke of the proud: v. 21

III. **ESTABLISH OUR DECISION:** vv. 22-24

   1. In spite of scorn, we will be faithful: v. 22.
   2. In spite of slander, we are strengthened: v. 23.
   3. In spite of sadness and loneliness, we will submit
      to God's Word: v. 24

This section of Psalm 119 challenges us to grapple with and recognize reality. God is the only one who knows what reality is and who can help us wrestle with the reality of our frustrations and problems.

The psalmist makes three practical suggestions that can assist us here. First, we need to examine our dependence upon God. The bottom line of verses 17-19 is that we desperately need God in our lives. Instead of pretending that we can do it ourselves, and that there is a "sacred" part of life and a "secular," and that God can take care of the sacred while we tend to the secular, we must recognize and examine our dependence upon God. When we really face reality, we realize we are, in fact, dependent upon God. Everything we need and desire ultimately will come from His hand.

In the Christian context, we can never achieve anything spiritually in our strength. Jesus declared, "You can do nothing without me." Nothing plus nothing equals nothing. Whatever we are able to achieve depends on God's smile.

We are dependent upon God for life itself. "Deal bountifully with thy servant, that I may live and keep thy word" (v. 17). Life is more than existence. Life is receiving the merciful blessings of God upon our lives and beings. The objective of life for the Christian is to "keep" the Word of God, ". . . that I may live and keep thy word." That is the ultimate goal for the Christian. The purpose of the Christian, in this life, is to glorify God. We find our greatest fulfillment in our relationship with God as we give Him glory. We are to reflect His beauty, His holiness, His character, as light in a dark world.

Remember Paul's words as he addressed pagan philosophers, "For in him we live, and move, and have our being" (Acts 17:28*a*). We are dependent upon God for every breath we draw, for every moment of life. James expressed it: "Every good gift and every perfect gift is from above, and cometh down from the Father of lights, with whom there is no variableness, neither shadow of turning" (Jas. 1:17). Paul wrote ". . . That ye walk worthy of the vocation wherewith ye are called" (Eph. 4:1). We have a distinct calling from God. That is our purpose in life.

Second, we are dependent upon God for insight into His Word. "Open thou mine eyes, that I may behold wondrous things out of thy law" (v. 2). The Bible is objectively the Word of God. Subjectively, my understanding of the Bible has to be enlightened by the Holy Spirit if I am to relate myself properly to the truth of the Word of God. The psalmist does not complain about the obscurity of the law. He does not protest to God, "You didn't make Yourself clear. You need to give us a plainer Word." Rather, he prays that the Lord will open his eyes that he can see what is there. That is the best way to approach Scripture—with a prayer that God will give one insight into His word.

Notice, he does not ask for any new revelation. He has less than half the Bible that we have, and yet what God has spoken is enough. He merely needs eyes to see it. We hear plenty today about "new revelation." There is no new revelation from God. There are *new insights* into the Word of God, but there is no new revelation. That is cultic or occultic and is against God. If we approach the Word of God as the psalmist did, God will bless us in a very special way. What God had given him was sufficient. He just wants to behold the marvels of the law. We are dependent upon God for insight into His Word. In 2 Corinthians 3, beginning at verse 13, Paul talked about Moses and the children of Israel. He wrote that there was a veil, a blinder, on the eyes of the children of Israel. Nevertheless, when they turned to the Lord, He removed the veil. When we beseech God, He makes His word clear to us. The simple issue is: Do we read the Bible for information or for instruction? There is a big difference.

Three Russians were presented to an Inerrancy Conference. Before that conference they expressed amazement that we would be discussing positions on the Scripture. In Russia, they simply read the Word of God to obey it. Do we read it for information and to draw conclusions about it, or do we read it for instruction? Do we read it to obey it? We are dependent on God for insight, and our obedience and our submission to Him make it possible for God to give us the insight we need to understand it. The Holy Spirit will open our eyes if we want Him to, but we are totally dependent upon God for insight into His Word.

We are also dependent upon God for guidance through life. "I am a stranger in the earth: hide not thy commandments from me" (v. 19). The idea of a pilgrim or a stranger runs throughout all of Scripture. The walk through this world is described as a pilgrimage. The psalmist avers openly, "I am a stranger here." Believers will always be strangers on the earth. We are not at home in any kingdom of this world. We are not at home in any religious kingdom, any political kingdom, any material kingdom. We are not at home here. That will always be the case. Like Abraham, we have no permanent dwelling place here. The admonition for us is not to tie ourselves to the things of this world. In a strange world, we need a guide. If we don't know the way, if we are in a strange place, we need a guide. We haven't gone in this direction before. We need a guide to lead us through the tight, precarious places. That is what the Word of God is. It guides us through those precarious places.

Elizabeth Elliott, before she married Jim Elliott and when she was a missionary in Ecuador, wrote that one day two North Americans showed up at her door and wanted her to teach them some Indian phrases. They were going into the jungles of Ecuador, and they wanted to have a few words they could speak to the Indians. They had everything they needed. They had cameras, snake boots, and the like, but the one indispensable item they needed to survive those upper Amazon jungles was a guide. If we are to survive the jungles of a strange world, we must have a guide. We are dependent upon God to guide us in this life. "Thy Word is a lamp unto my feet and a light unto my path" (Psalm 119:105). Our first action in facing reality is to examine our dependence for light, insight into His word, and for guidance in this life.

Secondly, we need to express our desire. "My soul breaketh for the longing that it hath unto thy judgments at all times" (v. 20). The word "breaketh" literally means "crushed" or "consumed." "My soul is crushed, my soul is consumed with your judgments. . . ." In other words, the psalmist's longing, his consuming passion lies in the contents of God's Word, God's statutes, God's teachings. He is motivated by two factors. He has already mentioned one. *He is motivated by the recognition of his own humanity.* He cannot make it by himself. That is one reason he desires to know the judgments of God. *The second is found in verse 21 when he has seen God's rebuke of the proud.* He has viewed the judgment of God upon the proud, how God brings down the proud, how He does not regard the arrogant—and the psalmist wants no part of that. So he prays, "I am consumed with the longing of your judgments at all times." He does not see himself as an exception to the rule, an exception to those who go astray of God's commands. He wants to be protected from God's judgments. He reasons that as long as he desires to hear, understand, and obey the commands of God, he feels he will be protected from the wrath of God.

If we have a high view of what God has told us to do and a proper approach to God's law, it leads us to an urgent desire to know the law of God and to obey it. We should continually desire to know the mind of God. What does God say to us? What does God want us to do? There ought to be a desire in our hearts to walk more closely with God. We ought to identify with Paul who said, after thirty years of being a Christian, "The desire of my life is that I may know Him." He knew the Lord as Savior, but he longed to know him better. That was the driving passion of his life. If we are going to face reality, we must do that by understanding that we need to express our desire to know the Word of God and the truth of God, and to be obedient to it.

Third, it follows logically: If we are going to face reality, we must establish our decision. "Remove from me reproach and contempt, for I have kept thy testimonies" (v. 22). He has made up his mind to be obedient to God. The greatest choice we can ever make is to be obedient to God, to stop playing and toying with being a Christian. God has a purpose and a will for our lives. He is not obscure about it. If we obey what we understand to do, God will give us new light, open up new vistas of understanding and new doors of opportunity. God will lead us from our obedience. *In spite of scorn, the psalmist declared he was going to be faithful.* When we are scorned and ridiculed by people, it is hard to bear. Such is a sorrow, indeed a heavy burden to bear. God will lift the distress and honor our decision to keep His commandments. It may be a painful and heavy yoke, the psalmist indicates, but he had made his decision. We must come to the place where even if folks laugh, ridicule, and put us to scorn, we have established our decision to keep the commandments of God.

I hear people remark, "I have tried obeying God, and it didn't work." How long did they try it? The kind of decision that has to be established is one of a lifetime. God alone can judge whether or not something works, because we only experience fleeting moments of reality. God grasps it in its entirety. God alone can judge whether a life is a success or a failure. When we reach heaven and the crowns are passed out, we probably will not have heard about most who receive those crowns. They will be missionaries who served in the shadows, inner-city pastors and deacons who labored, and few knew or cared about them. They will be people who never garnered publicity, never appeared on television, never wrote a book, or the like, but they established a commitment to obey God.

It was a lifetime commitment. They didn't turn away from it, they didn't become scared, and give in to the pressures. They established their decision and, like the psalmist, in spite of scorn they were faithful. If we make that kind of commitment, God will carry us on from there. Most of us want to know God's will so we can consider it. God doesn't operate like that. "In spite of scorn, God; in spite of ridicule, I am going to keep Your commandments." Nobody can make us disobey God. They may pressure us, they may scoff at us and ridicule us, but they cannot make us disobey God. The psalmist does not care what they do. He has made his decision. God is looking for people who will establish this kind of decision.

"Princes also did sit and speak against me: but thy servant did mediate in thy statutes" (v. 23). The word "sit" suggests that they were securely settled. He had already talked about being a stranger. People who have accepted that they have to settle down and be at home in this world are speaking against him. People who do not have eternity in mind, who do not see past the temporary moments, people to whom ultimate reality is a two-car garage with two new cars, a prestigious position, a huge house, and whatever else they think they want, have bought into the world system. Christians are just as guilty of that as all others.

In the latest Congress on Evangelism that Billy Graham chaired in Amsterdam, Jon Moore spent considerable time with people from one of the Eastern European Communist countries. Their burden for their country was that the Christians had become too materialistic. There they were with the one suit they owned and old shoes, yet they were concerned they had become too materialistic. We have settled down and made peace with the enemy. We have established detente with Satan himself. Those who have established that security, sit and speak against God.

In spite of slander, though, the psalmist says he is going to be faithful. The enemy recognizes the greatness in God's people, and he is envious. The most miserable person in this world is Satan. He has more power than any human being could ever muster; he knows the Bible; he knows the end; and he is miserable. And we think Satan can give us something to make us happy. Satan looks at Christian people and envies their joy, their peace. So, he abuses, slanders, and lies about the believer and often succeeds in hurting him. Nothing hurts as much as to be slandered, to be lied about, and to be spoken against. Sadly, he finds many willing helpers, even in the Christian community.

Anytime we attack another believer, we are doing Satan's work for him. We are helping him out. Peace and solace are real as we meditate on the Word of God. ". . . But thy servant did meditate in thy statutes." If we want to have peace in the midst of the storm of opposition, of ridicule, and of slander, then meditate on the Word of God. In spite of slander we must be faithful.

"Thy testimonies also are my delight and my counsellors" (v. 24). There is a hint of sadness in this verse. *In spite of sadness and loneliness, we should submit to the Word of God.* It is as though he is saying, "There is no one else to delight in; there is no one else I can call a counsellor. There is no one else I trust enough to pour my heart out to. So, thy testimonies are also my delight and my counsellors." Though we are sad or lonely many times, we submit to the Word of God, to His counsel, and His delight found in the Word of God. That is consistently the message of Scripture. "Thou wilt keep him in perfect peace whose mind is stayed on thee, because he trusteth in thee" (Isa. 26:3). "Thou wilt shew me the path of life: in they presence is fulness of joy; at thy right hand there are pleasures for evermore" (Psalm 16:11). God doesn't shortchange us. He gives us the best. In spite of loneliness or sadness that may come upon us because of our stand for God, we will continue to submit to the Word of God because there is our strength, our solace, our commitment.

If we can reach the place where we establish our decision to be obedient to God, not caring what anybody else says, then we can accept God's definition of reality and find victory in it. Or, we can spend our lives looking for answers, never finding one that is enough. God is reality. Let's establish our decision for Him.

4

Strength for Weak Days

Psalm 119:25-32

I. **MY WAYS:** vv. 25-29

   1. Confession: v. 25
   2. Conviction: vv. 26-27
   3. Contradiction: vv. 28-29

II. **THY WAYS:** vv. 30-32

   1. Choice: v. 30
   2. Commitment: v. 31
   3. Celerity: v. 32

The psalmist is crying from the crucible of affliction. He is having difficulties in his personal life. He is a believer, but he is struggling, seeking deeper understanding and insight into the Word of God. That in itself ought to encourage us because we all come to the place, particularly if we are regular and faithful in church, where we feel as if we ought to be stronger. We ought to be better and more in control in our Christian walk. There ought to be more victory than we sometimes experience, and at times Satan uses that to beat us down.

The psalmist is going through precisely that in these verses. He is making God his confidant. That is always a good practice because God always gives a gracious response when we come to Him. He is always open to the approach of individuals. He wants to be in our lives, giving us insight and understanding, far more than we desire it. The psalmist's problems do not drive him away from God but drive him toward God. The difficulties, problems, and discouragements we face will either drive us to God or away from Him.

The psalmist's difficulties are a result of sin and weaknesses in his life. He is facing the truth about himself. This section of the psalm divides into two parts: my ways and God's ways. Truthfully, there are only two ways to do anything, my ways and God's ways. We will either do it our way or God's way. It can be defined otherwise philosophically, but basically it boils down to these two concepts.

> My soul cleaveth unto the dust: quicken thou me according to thy word. I have declared my ways, and thou heardest me: teach me thy statutes. Make me to understand the way of thy precepts: so shall I talk of thy wondrous works. My soul melteth for heaviness: strengthen thou me according unto thy word. Remove from me the way of lying: and grant me thy law graciously (vv. 25-29).

In verse 25 we are confronted with a confession. "My soul cleaves unto the dust" could be translated literally, "My soul is bowed in mourning, in grief, in sorrow." The complaint is the language of conflict, of humiliation, not despondency. He is not only depressed, he is guilty. He is facing his own sinfulness, the grief and sorrow his choices have brought into his life. He is not just depressed and wanting someone to talk to. He knows full well that the problems he is facing are derived from his pursuit of his way. We have that right. We will always mess up if we do, and we will always be sad. We will never find fulfillment if we go our way. Thus, the psalmist is describing for us the discouragement and despair of doing it "our way."

"I have declared my ways" (v. 26) is a confession. This confession is the beginning of his restoration, of the return to his fellowship with the Lord. It is the beginning of his return to spiritual sanity. This confession is the beginning of the stirring of God in his life. The tragedy is that the world has such power over us. "My ways," the way the world thinks, have tremendous control over us. We are so dead to spiritual things. Even those of us who come regularly to the sanctuary to hear the Word of God are in the throes of such onerous control by the world. We are so insensitive to spiritual truth. This writer admitted that.

It is a deeply sincere confession. He is simply acknowledging the truth about himself. If we will be honest with God, He will respond to us. He demands honesty of people who come to Him. Tell Him the truth. He knows it anyway! Remember that Jesus had a man contact Him one day about healing his son. Jesus said, "Do you believe I can do it?" And his answer was, "Lord, I believe, help thou mine unbelief." What a rinky-dink answer that was! But Jesus healed the son. That is perplexing until we realize the man was just being honest. If we will be honest with God, we will always find God graciously responding to us. That is the essence of confession. It is admitting what God already knows. We do not inform God when we confess—we agree with Him. Here is an honest and sincere confession of "my ways." "This is how I am."

He has a conviction: ". . . And thou heardest me: teach me thy statutes. Make me to understand the way of thy precepts: so shall I talk of thy wondrous works" (vv. 26*b*-27). He has a conviction that God listened to his prayer and responded and what his response needs to be. Whenever we are honest in confessing what God already knows, we always gain new insights into the marvelous words and works of God. Whenever we give confession, we have better understanding of His Word. The trouble with most of us is we want to have understanding for information. We just want to know what it says. We don't have a particular desire to do it— we just want to understand it. We don't realize that until we are ready to respond to what God reveals, we won't understand much about His word. This man confessed, and God gave him insight.

In verses 28 and 29 we are faced with a contradiction. The psalmist has made his confession and declared his conviction, and here is a contradiction. "My soul melteth for heaviness:

strengthen thou me according unto thy word. Remove from me the way of lying: and grant me thy law graciously" (vv. 28-29). The contradiction is that, in spite of his past experience with God, he is still heavy in his heart, and in his soul he is still given to the way of lying. The "way of lying" is any deviation from the will and Word of God in our lives. It is anytime we choose our way over God's way. Here is a man who has made his confession and expressed his conviction, and yet his life is still a contradiction to what he claims to believe. Is that true with us? We know the right things. We believe the right things. We know God has saved us. We seek God, and yet there is still that contradiction.

As long as we are living, abiding, and responding to "my way," we are going to be a living contradiction. It is a contradiction for us to stand, sing, praise, and pray on Sunday and then live like the devil during the week. It is a contradiction for us to claim we have given ourselves to God and not demonstrate it in every area of our lives. It is a contradiction to affirm that we love God, but we hate our brothers and sisters in this life. "My way" is a contradictory way. The way that is against God's way is always going to be full of contradictions.

This "melting of heaviness" is not complete until it has bowed us before God. "O God, strengthen me according to thy word." He saw his contradiction. Seeing how his heart melted under the awareness of his inadequacy and the contradictory life he was living, he bowed before God and cried, "O God, strengthen me according to thy word. Remove from me the way of lying: and grant me thy law graciously" (vv. 28b-29). Any departure in principle and conduct from God's way is "my way." If we will allow it, understanding that we are going our way instead of God's way, we can finally bow before God and say, "Strengthen me, remove the way of lying from me and grant me your law graciously."

The last verses in this section speak of "thy way," God's ways. Verses 29 and 30 gives us these two choices: the way of lying and the way of truth. There are only two choices—the way of man and the way of God. My ways, His ways.

In verse 30 is a choice. "I have chosen the way of truth." It is a deliberate choice he has exercised to follow God. It is vital for all of us as Christians continually to reach the place where we declare that we have chosen God's way, the way of truth. We have chosen to let God be the Governor of our lives, to let Him send us and use us any way He desires. Choose the way of truth. Everything else is deceptive, less than what it appears. The way of the world cannot deliver, cannot fulfill its promises. God's way is the only one in which there is meaning and purpose in life.

Will we choose man's way or will we choose God's way? The psalmist sang, "I have chosen the way of truth." We are so small in our thinking. Most of us never think God would send us to Argentina, Africa, Afghanistan, etc. Why not? If He wants anybody he might want us. And we know He wants somebody. Why not us? Why not make up our minds that we are not going to limit God by giving parameters in which we will serve Him. We give Him options, and then ask Him what He wants us to do within these options.

What we ought to do is say, "God, I have made a choice. I have chosen the way of truth. If it means living on the backside of the desert with nobody ever knowing where I am or hearing from me again, Lord, I am choosing Your way. Whatever it means, Lord, if that is what You want me to do, then that is what I want to do." The psalmist understood that kind of limitation on God is man's way. He had already proven that doesn't work. "My soul cleaves to the dust." He is saying, "I am about to die." He has been doing it his way. Man's way is always like that. "I have chosen not the way of lying, but of truth. That is my choice," the psalmist said. We all have that choice, the choice to give God narrow parameters, then to define what we are willing to do, and finally ask Him what He wants us to do within the confines of those narrow restrictions. Or we can say, "The field is the world, wherever You want me to go, whatever You want me to do, I will do it." *We have a choice to follow God's way.*

More than that, we have a commitment. "I have stuck unto thy testimonies: O Lord, put me not to shame" (v. 31). There is a difference between a choice and a commitment. If we make a choice, we intellectually assent to something as being true. If we make a commitment, we put our life on the line.

When I was young I heard about a man who pushed a wheelbarrow, loaded with a 200-pound sack of sand, across a tightwire over Niagara Falls. The crowds cheered. When asked how many thought he could push a man across, they cheered louder. But when he asked for volunteers no one spoke a word. There is a difference between choosing to believe something as truth and committing yourself to it. We can claim all day that we are choosing God's way. That is a choice. "I have clung to Your testimonies." That is not only a passive choice but an active commitment. It is not just an acknowledgment of truth, but of trust. First choosing, then sticking to it. Too many of us have made a choice but have not made a commitment, and we have wondered why we are frustrated. God wants us to choose His way. That certainly is the right choice. But He also wants us to commit ourselves to doing what He tells us to do. Our prayer for understanding the Word of God is useless unless we have made a commitment to trust. The gap between choice and commitment is often extremely wide.

When Noah Webster compiled his first dictionary for the American people several hundred years ago he included the word "celerity." The word speaks of velocity, speed. He used the illustration of a bird's speed like a falcon or hawk as it soars and dips down toward the earth. It speaks of rapid motion and the velocity of a bullet. If we make a *choice* to do it God's way, and we made a *commitment* to do it God's way, the next step is to do it with *celerity,* swiftly. "I will *run* the way of thy commandments, when thou shalt enlarge my heart" (v. 32).

The devil's greatest tool is to give us reasons to procrastinate. "I can't serve Jesus, I am still in school." "I can't serve Jesus, my kids are taking all of my time." We are living right now. Don't put it off until another day because the devil can always supply you with a reason to put it off. If we are going to do God's will, we must do it with celerity. Do it right now! We are not waiting for a day that has not yet come, for a time when we will "arrive." We are living right now, and we need to choose God's way, commit ourselves to God's way, and get on with it.

And in doing that, God will "enlarge his heart." Most scholars will agree that the concept of enlarging the heart means to gain more understanding. That is the whole context of this passage. The psalmist wants a word from God in the midst of the weaknesses, problems, and afflictions he is enduring. This "running in the way of God's commandments" implies more than an apathetic following. It speaks of an eagerness in following the prescribed course. The more he pursues the things of God, the more God will broaden his understanding of His ways.

The reason God's ways are so foreign to most of us is that we don't walk in His ways. We would understand God better if we would just obey him, if we would put ourselves under His control. When we trust without understanding, God brings understanding. But the trust must come first. All of us want to understand the Word of God more. If we obey it, we will understand it more. If we live up to the light we have, the understanding we have, God will give us more understanding. The best way to understand the way of God and the Word of God is to be obedient to God. Run to do His Word. Run to obey Him. The happiest people are those who cling more closely to God, even when they are bowed with grief and affliction, even when their souls cleave unto the dust, even when their souls melt for heaviness.

We will not have a choice as to whether we will endure affliction. We *will* endure affliction. Our only choice is what we will do when affliction comes. Most of our afflictions we bring upon ourselves. I can go back in my life and realize the times I was the most depressed were when I was the most stupid, when I did some "dumb things." The psalmist understood that he had caused most of his problems. But instead of letting his problems make him bitter toward God and drive him away from God, he let them drive him toward God. That should happen in all of our lives. We may

not understand what God is saying; we may not comprehend
the way of God in our circumstance, but we are still going to
trust Him. My way—nothing but despair, affliction, problems.
God's way—strength, truth, understanding. Let's move out
with celerity . . . now.

5

Looking at Something Lasting

Psalm 119:33-40

I. **PERCEPTION:** vv. 33-35

    1. Instruction: v. 33
    2. Intensity: v. 34
    3. Inspiration: v. 35

II. **PREOCCUPATION:** vv. 36-37

    1. Dishonesty: v. 36
    2. Deception: v. 37

III. **PRIORITIES:** vv. 38-40

    1. Reverence: v. 38
    2. Reproach: v. 39
    3. Revival: v. 40

The theme running through this section is a request for guidance and understanding, for such an understanding of the Word of God that we will be thrust into action. It is a plea not only for intellectual understanding but for it to be translated into ethical, moral, and spiritual action on our part. More than just a cry for understanding and guidance, there is also the clear call for us to focus on eternal things and not the temporary things of this life. It is a warning for us to stay away from covetousness and vanity, and a challenge to love God rather than the world.

There are three basic sections to this passage. *In verses 33*

through 35 the psalmist is calling for a perception. He wants understanding and insight, a perception into the truth of the Word of
God. In verses 36 through 37, he warns us of a preoccupation with
the things of this world. In the last verses, 38 through 40, he calls
us to have the proper priorities for our lives.

The Perception: "Teach me, O Lord, the way of thy statues; and
I shall keep it unto the end" (v. 33). *The psalmist is crying out for
instruction, for God to teach him how to put into practice the statutes of God*. If we are to live like God wants us to live, He has to
teach us. We don't need any instruction in sin! That comes naturally. We are sinners by nature, by choice, by conduct. It is natural
for us to be disobedient to God. It is call "original sin," "total
depravity." It doesn't necessarily mean we are as bad as we can
be—it means we have a tendency to sin. The psalmist understands
we must be instructed in the things of God. If we are to live and
respond as God would have us respond, we need instruction. The
darkness needs to be removed from our eyes. It matters not how
bright the sun is at noonday if a blind man is trying to see. If he is
to see, the optic nerves must be stimulated to the point they perceive. The psalmist is praying that God will remove the darkness
which keeps him from perceiving, and teach him His statutes.

The little phrase "the end" means, first of all, the end of life.
But it also means "to the fullness of obedience," to obey God
perfectly. Very simply, we will keep the law of God, the Word of
God, as long as we breath. As we do it, we will become accustomed to doing it and God will lead us to do it completely.

"Give me understanding, and I shall keep thy law; yea, I shall
observe it with my whole heart" (v. 34). *He not only prays for
perception but also that he will act with intensity*. "Whole heart"
means enthusiastically. The psalmist says he is going to keep the
law with all of his energy, all of his ability. That is how we ought
to serve God. There ought to be an intensity about our service for
God. How can we be intense about everything else in life and yet
yawn our way through church and our devotional time. There
needs to be a real sense of conviction and action. For most of us,

there is a large gap between what we believe and how we live.

"Make me to go in the path of thy commandments; for therein do I delight" (v. 35). He introduces a concept here that we should not only do what God commands, but we ought to delight in doing it. Jesus tells us, "For my yoke is easy and my burden is light" (Matt. 11:30). The devil tells us it is hard to serve Jesus, that it is burdensome. But the Word of God tells us it is not heavy. Rather, it is a delight to obey God. Whatever pleasure there may be in sin, the greatest pleasure in life is in being obedient to God. The psalmist wants to have the experience not only of obeying God but obeying Him *because he wants to obey Him.* The only obedience that God accepts is that which is given, not that which is forced.

This profound prayer for perception is, "Teach me Your way. Instruct me in Your statutes and make me go in the path of Your commandments, and I am going to delight in doing it with my whole heart!"

Then the psalmist warns us about preoccupation. "Incline my heart unto thy testimonies, and not to covetousness. Turn away mine eyes from beholding vanity; and quicken thou me in thy way" (vv. 36-37). There are two kinds of preoccupations. One is covetousness, and the other is vanity. *First, he warns about dishonesty.* "Incline my heart . . ." We have two choices. We either turn our hearts toward the Word of God or toward covetousness, material pursuit. We focus on the things of this life or on the things of God. That is our only choice. The psalmist says, "Incline my heart unto your testimonies. Don't incline it toward covetousness."

I think of a fork in the road. One is the Word of God, the other, covetousness. One is spirituality, the other, materialism. One is eternity, the other, temporal things. We can and do become preoccupied with these things. First, this passage says it is dishonest to keep the testimonies of God without inclining our heart to Him. God wants our inclined heart loving and serving Him. He doesn't just want us blindly to keep His commandments. He has angels who do that, and do whatever they are told. We are not only to do what He commands us to do, but we are to do it because our heart is turned toward Him.

At this point many Christians are miserable in their Christian walk. Many of us are doing the "right things," but they aren't working. What is wrong? Perhaps we are merely keeping rules and regulations without turning our hearts toward God. If we turn our hearts toward God, we understand that God is God and can do whatever He wants with our lives. We are in a very self-centered, "me-type" generation which contends if we serve God, all our prayers will be answered like we want them to be and we will have no problems, and if we keep His Word, He will automatically keep us from harm. What many are doing is keeping all the laws and commands of God without turning their hearts toward God. If we turn our hearts toward God, we will be content with what He gives us; we will long for His presence in our lives more than anything else.

It is dishonest to keep His commands without turning our hearts toward Him. If we do that, we will be led into covetousness. Covetousness is a focusing on the things of this life—on pleasure and comfort, and the attainments, power, and prestige of this life. Covetousness is idolatry because it dethrones God and places ourselves upon the throne. It is selfishness of the highest degree and destroys everything it touches. It is a sordid greed that would sell even the Lord Jesus Himself, as Judas did. It is degrading, deadening, and destructive of everything it touches. I can think of no principle so destructive of our relationship with God as covetousness. It destroys our obedience because the love of God and the love of the world cannot live in the same heart.

The desire for material things is proof of our unfaithfulness to God. Jesus made it plain: "You cannot serve two masters" (Matt. 6:24). Many of us are trying to serve two masters. We are preoccupied with the world. Our brand of faith is not demanding, not costly. It is almost totally self-centered. The bottom line is that it shuns authority. The secular world and much of the religious world do not want to acknowledge the authority of God in our lives, because we want to focus on the things of this world. It leads us to a preoccupation with covetousness.

In 1983, Alexander Solzshenitsyn, the Russian dissident, was awarded the Templeton Laureate Award for his contribution to the world of religion. Solzshenitsyn is an outspoken critic of the Soviet system and a very committed Christian. He had much to say about life behind the "Iron Curtain." When he accepted the Templeton Award, he made a speech in which he gave tremendous attention to the atheistic culture of Russia today and how it had attempted to stamp out the people's understanding of God, how the government had destroyed the church buildings, how they had removed the opportunities of the Christian to advance, and described in detail the very ungodly system in the Soviet Union today. Then he addressed himself to us. In part, he declared:

> Unnoticeably, through decades of gradual erosion, the meaning of life in the West ceased to stand for anything more lofty than the pursuit of happiness which is also protected under the Constitution. The concepts of good and evil have been ridiculed for several centuries. Banished from common use, they have been replaced by political or class considerations of short-lived value. It has become embarrassing to appeal to eternal concepts, embarrassing to state that evil makes its home in the individual heart before it enters a political system. Yet, it is not considered shameful to make daily concessions to an integral evil. Judging by the continuing landslide of concessions made before the eyes of our very own generation, the West is inevitably slipping toward the abyss. Let us ask ourselves, "Are not the ideals of our century false?" Our life consists not in the pursuit of material success but in the quest of worthy spiritual growth. Our entire earthly existence is but a transitional stage in the movement toward something higher, and we must not stumble and fall. Nor must we linger fruitlessly on one rung of the ladder. Material laws alone do not explain our life and give it direction. The laws of physics and physiology will never reveal the indisputable manner in which the Creator constantly, day

in and day out, participates in the life of each of us, unfailingly granting us the energy of existence. When this existence leaves us, we die. In the life of our entire planet, the Divine Spirit moves with no less force. This we must grasp in our dark and terrible hour.

His is a solemn and eloquent plea to us in the Western World not to be preoccupied with the temporal things of this life: covetousness, focusing on material and earthly pursuits.

Second, the psalmist warns us not to be preoccupied with deception. "Turn away mine eyes from beholding vanity" (v. 37). Vanity means in Hebrew what it does in English—that which is hollow, shallow, trivial, insignificant, worthless, that which may glitter but has no fulfillment. Don't give yourself over to the deception of vain things. It is tragic when an individual spends his entire life captivated by trivial pursuits.

Not long ago one of our church families had their house burn to the ground. Visiting with the husband, I asked how much they had lost. Everything was lost but he went on to remark, "We really lost nothing. We lost some things that will be old and worthless anyway, but we lost nothing that really counts." Many people spend their lives focused on material things, and an accident or tragedy destroys everything they have lived for. When we are preoccupied with dishonest and deceptive things, we are at the mercy of what happens to us. The psalmist is pleading for us not to make the mistake of being preoccupied with those things that cannot give us happiness, fulfillment, meaning, or purpose.

"Turn away mine eyes from beholding vanity." Do you realize how often we are led astray by what we look at? The psalmist doesn't say, "Shut your eyes." Many of us have the "ostrich-in-the-sand" concept. If we don't see it, it doesn't happen. Rather, he writes, be sure you are looking at the right object. Turn your eyes away from temporary, sensual things that are emotional and soon gone. Watch what you look at. Your eyes are the windows of your soul. What you look at will find lodging in your heart. No individual who ever committed immorality did it until he began to watch and look at things that should not have been observed. How we use our eyes is important.

No individual who was ever guilty of dishonesty, embezzling, and/or stealing, did it until first he began to view things he desired. Some of us focus our attention on these transitory, vain things more than the things that really count. That is the reason for much of the frustration and unhappiness we experience. If we incline our hearts and focus our eyes on eternal considerations, nothing can happen to destroy our happiness and satisfaction. God guides us through life with victory.

Then the psalmist calls us to the right kind of priorities in these last three verses. "Stablish thy word unto thy servant, who is devoted to thy fear." The first priority is reverence, fear. The fear of God, the awe of God. Notice he says, ". . . The servant who is devoted to thy fear." To be devoted to the fear of God is to be obsessed with God, with who God is. It is to be in awe of God. God is not our "buddy," not the "Man Upstairs." God is God, and we ought to come with awe into His presence. With Jesus we can come boldly, but we never lose the sense of reverence and awe. We come boldly before Him, knowing He hears us, that anything asked in His will He gives us. We come boldly because we have access into the Holy Place through Jesus Christ, but we never come with lightheartedness, with levity, casually, or carelessly because we come obsessed with who God is. If we are obsessed with the fear of God, we will be delivered from the fear of other things, and we will not be distressed with the fear of other things.

"Turn away my reproach which I fear: for thy judgments are good" (v. 39). There is a reproach for which we ought to be grateful. When we are suffering for Jesus' sake, we should be thankful for that kind of reproach. Someone identifies us with Jesus and places us alongside the people of God, and we bear the reproach of Christ. That is a "good" reproach; we ought to seek it. But there is a reproach we should shun, the reproach of bringing dishonor to the name of God. The psalmist never wants to be a disgrace to God. He is afraid to embarrass Him. If the psalmist is David, rightly he should fear it. Remember in 2 Samuel 12 when Nathan the prophet confronted David with the sin of his adultery with Bathsheba, his murder of Uriah, and all that was involved, David confessed, in verse 13, "I have sinned against the Lord." He owned up to his sin, but Nathan answered, "That is fine, but you will have to suffer the consequences, because by this deed you have given great occasion to the enemies of the Lord to blaspheme. You have given God's enemies a chance to laugh at God. You are a reproach to God."

No wonder the psalmist sang, "Protect me from the reproach which I fear." All of us ought to fear that kind of reproach and shun the reproach that could bring dishonor to the name of Christ. Our trouble is that we are preoccupied with our "rights." But we have no right to disgrace God. If we name the name of Jesus Christ, we have no right to be an embarrassment to Him. Paul wrote, "Ye are not your own . . . ye are bought with a price" (1 Cor. 6:19-20). He paid for everything about us. We belong to Him. If you are a professing Christian and you feel you have the right to dishonor God, then probably you have never been saved. If you have dishonored God, and it grieved you, and you knew it was wrong, then that is evidence of God's presence in your life. But if you think you can go laughing through life, disregarding God's will and disobeying God's commands, and live like the devil, you are a disgrace to God, and you have no right to do that.

"Keep me from the reproach that I fear." He feared that once again he might be a disgrace, a dishonor to God, and because of what he did, the enemies of God might blaspheme Him. Our priority ought to be that we never dishonor God.

Then he prays for revival. That ought to be another priority for us. He uses the word "quicken" twice in this passage, first in verse 37 and then in verse 40. ". . . Quicken me in thy righteousness." He pleads for the quickening power of God in his life, but he doesn't do it too often. One can't ask God too often to revive him. We need it every hour, every day. We need God to restore us, to revive us, to draw our hearts to Him. Sadly, we are so prone to apathy, to indifference. We become calloused and numbed to the things to God.

Despite the huge numbers of evangelical Christians in America, our vital organs are slowly, but surely, being destroyed. The most vivid memory I have of wildlife in East Africa is the frightened gazelle or impala whose eyes read stark terror, still alive, while a preying lion of the savannah was eating its insides. Alive, yet dead. The insides of the animal being gnawed yet the eyes and the brain still functioning! One of the most tragic pictures I have ever seen. I am afraid we are seeing that in evangelical Christianity today. There is still life, but there is a sense of terror that something is horribly wrong. While there is some evidence of life, the vital organs of American Christianity are being slowly gnawed away.

The psalmist says it is not enough just to know what to do. He prays for understanding and guidance, but he says, "Oh, God, make me to go in Your way. Quicken me with Your spirit."

The Word of God is very instrumental in this process. God's Word and quickening have an undeniable link. The obedience to the Word of God and revival have been seen all the way from Moses to the present day. But until Biblical knowledge is galvanized into action, our world will remain unreached, and our faith will continue to wane.

Knowing the truth is not enough. Dead orthodoxy is not the answer. We can believe all the right things, give affirmation to all the right truths, make an A+ on all the orthodoxy tests, and still be dead as a door nail. The answer is for us to be so involved in our relationship to the Lord and so committed to Him that He works in us, causing us to obey Him, not because we have to but because we want to. To love him with all of our hearts and fix our attention on Him, not on those things that pass away, is the answer.

During the Second World War, a soldier lay in an army hospital. His right arm had been severed in the heat of battle. One of the officers stopped to visit with the young man in the hospital. While talking to him, the officer remarked, "I am sorry that you lost your arm."

The young man looked up with his eyes ablaze and replied, "Sir, I didn't lose it, I gave it." There is a difference. We can spend our lives losing the things we fix our attention on, losing our reputation, our possessions, our positions, our power, our prestige, our relationships—and spend all our lifetime moaning about what we have lost. But if we want to know the essence of vital, vibrant faith, it is a faith that has already given away everything to the Lord. When it is all His, we don't lose something—we give something.

If He owns it all, it is all His, none of ours. Then we go through life with joy and with confidence as He shows us His will, His Word. We do it not because He forces us to do it, but because we choose to do it. We obey because we love Him, and He gives us the fulfillment of every desire of our hearts. But it only comes when our hearts are quickened and our eyes are focused on him . . . but it does come.

There is no joy in blind obedience. The joy ensues when we turn our hearts and eyes toward Him. We obey Him because He is the object of our concentration, our affection.

This is the prayer: "Give us perception, Oh, Lord, keep us from being preoccupied with covetousness and vanity. May our priorities be to reverence You, not to be a reproach to Your name, and to experience You in our hearts."

6

Walking in Liberty

Psalm 119:41-48

I. **DIVINELY EQUIPPED:** vv. 41-43

   1. Reception: v. 41
   2. Response: v. 42
   3. Responsibility: v. 43

II. **DIRECTLY ENABLED:** vv. 44-45

   1. Consistency: v. 44
   2. Constraint: v. 45

III. **DISTINCTLY EXHIBITED:** vv. 46-48

   1. Determination: v. 46
   2. Delight: v. 47
   3. Demonstration: v. 48

Verses 41 through 48 is an unusual section of Psalm 119 because it doesn't seem to have much continuity. The reason is easily understood. Each of the Hebrew words that divide this psalm represent a different letter of the Hebrew alphabet. Each of the eight verses of each section begins with that letter. The Hebrew letter for this section is one for which there are few Hebrew words. The English equivalent to the Hebrew word that begins this section is "and." It is hard to do much with "and" and have it tie together.

What we have here is a series of six promises and two petitions.

In these eight verses are two *prayers* or requests to God and six *promises* to God. The thread that runs through and ties these verses together is a holy fear of God, a deep sense of awe and reverence for who God is and what God's presence is like. It describes what we are to be in the light of God's presence.

These verses are really one continual pleading. There is a spirit of petitioning that goes through the passage as the writer is praying for the abiding grace of God in his spirit and in his soul. He supports his requests with a profound spirit of burning love for God. We cannot read this passage without being aware of the love in the heart of the writer.

He prays for courage to give a strong testimony of the superlative truth of God's Word.

We all want to walk in the liberty that is ours in Jesus Christ. If that occurs, this passage points us to three evident things. *First, if we are to walk in liberty, we are going to be divinely equipped.* Whatever liberty is ours comes from God. It is given to us by God.

"Let thy mercies come also unto me, O Lord, even thy salvation, according to thy word. So shall I have wherewith to answer him that reproacheth me: for I trust in thy word. And take not the word of truth utterly out of my mouth; for I have hoped in thy judgments" (vv. 41-43). In verse 41 he speaks of receiving the mercies of the salvation of God. Notice he calls it "thy salvation." We speak a lot today about "my salvation." The psalm emphasizes particularly "thy salvation." Salvation is always attributed to God. It is not "my salvation" other than the fact that I have received the gift of God, but it is God's salvation. To be saved is to receive the life of God, the forgiveness of God, the grace of God into my life. The Word of God shows us the way of salvation. It promises us the salvation of God and describes for us the inward evidence and manifestation of salvation—and it is all tied up in the Lord Himself. It is God's salvation we are talking about. It is consistent with His Word.

Here is a prayer of profound anxiety and desire, and yet simple faith. The psalmist is literally saying, *"Let* your mercies come unto me."* Genuine faith is always simple, simple in that it has a single object. It is faith in God, faith in God's Word, faith in what God has revealed to us. Remember the ground of our faith is "according to thy word." How do we know what we believe? The Word of God! Everything we believe is according to the Word of God. If it is not in the Word of God, then I cannot build a system on it. This is the beautiful description of the ground of our faith.

At the beginning of this section, he is praying for the rich variety of the blessings of God and the mercies of God to fall upon him with the desired results that he will have the equipping to answer his enemies, those who would reproach him and his Lord.

One fact is sure. We will find reproach as Christians. There will be reproach from being identified with Christ. It is amazing that in our society today, any identification with Christ is treated with ridicule. The slander and attack of a secular world will bombard us. If you don't believe it, carry your Bible to work with you or wherever you go. Any identification with the things of God brings hostility and slander. That shouldn't surprise us. Jesus foretold, "They hated me. They are going to hate you. A servant is no better than his master. They will treat you the way they treated me."

The desire of the psalmist's heart is that he might have so much of the grace and salvation of God expressing itself in his life that he will have an answer to those who criticize him. "Whereas I was blind, now I see" is an unanswerable answer. The person who is not sure in his relationship with God, who doesn't walk in the Spirit and presence of God, doesn't have an answer when the world attacks him. The person who has experienced the salvation of God and His rich mercies coming upon his life will find that his very life is an answer. This is why Peter says, "It is the will of God that with well doing you might put to silence the ignorance of foolish men."

There are three kinds of critics for the Christian. There are the devil, the heretics, and the slanderers. The devil must be answered by an internal word of humility. The heretic must be answered by an external word of wisdom. The slanderer must be answered by an active word of conduct, by the way we live. Some years ago, under particularly trying circumstances, I found myself trying to defend myself. A dear friend said, "If you have to defend yourself, you have no defense." How do we defend ourselves? Not by our words, but by the kind of lives we lead. Our lives are an open book before the world, and people see and have the answer about a person who walks with the Lord. The psalmist is praying for this type of life-style.

There is another type of reproach we also bear. Not only criticism from those who are against the things of God, but from Satan himself. He throws doubts into our faces; he makes a mock of our helplessness, our guilt, our difficulties. It is a serious moment when we feel a sense of spiritual desertion. We feel isolated. In that moment, the psalmist is doubtlessly thinking of the reproach of the grand accuser himself, so the psalmist prays, "Let me have so much of an overflow of your mercies that when I am reproached, I will have an answer to him who reproaches me" (Author's paraphrase).

When we are reproached, when the critic arises, when the enemy comes, we can simply testify with the blind man, "I was blind, but now I see. I don't know much more, but I know that" (see John 9). The world cannot answer that answer. It is the answer of how God moves in our lives. We gain an answer to the reproacher by the rich mercies of God. The real answer is the presence of God in our lives. It is not that we have an answer to all the questions, not that we are able to out-debate those who throw their barbs at us, but that we have the reality of Jesus Christ, His salvation, living in us!

"And take not the word of truth utterly out of my mouth; for I have hoped in thy judgments" (v. 43). The word of truth is none other than the precepts of the Lord. Not to have them taken out of my mouth means not to be deprived of the opportunity of speaking to other people about them. He is saying, "I have built my hope on your Word. Now don't fail to give me an opportunity to tell others about it." That is the equipping of God upon the life of the believer—that we will make the most of the opportunity to witness to others what God has done in our lives.

It is not natural for us to enjoy the goodness of God and keep quiet about it. We don't do this in any other area of life. We seem to get excited about everything—except the Lord. It is OK to make an idiot of ourselves at a ball game. I remember growing up dreaming of the day Baylor would win a Southwest Conference championship. In 1974 when we beat Texas and started winning all our games, we played Rice in November. It was freezing cold and sleeting. Very few attended the game. We had already won the championship. I drove all the way to Waco. I sat forty rows up in the bleachers for one reason. I wanted to hear George Stokes announce, "Welcome to Baylor Stadium, home of the Southwest Conference Champion Baylor Bears." It wasn't too cold or too far away to hear that. It would have been unnatural for me to respond any other way. Growing up I bled Baylor green and gold and cherished all that goes with such loyalty.

We ought to have the same sense of freedom in responding to what we have received in Jesus Christ. The essence of the equipping of God the psalmist is praying for is: "Oh, God, give me a rich and full experience, and don't deprive me of the opportunity to tell others about it." The condition for free utterance is a rich encounter with Jesus Christ.

The reason we have so much trouble pumping people up to visit is because they haven't had the kind of encounter with the Lord that will make them want to share with other people. We ought to rejoice in our relationship with God.

So, if we are to walk in liberty, we must be divinely equipped. With the experience of the mercies of God, even the salvation of God, coming upon us according to the Word of God, we will have answers to those who reproach us because we are trusting in the Lord, and God won't take from us the opportunity to share it with others.

If we are going to walk in liberty, we will have to be directly enabled. "So shall I keep thy law continually for ever and ever. And I will walk at liberty: for I seek thy precepts" (vv. 44-45). The psalmist expresses in verse 44 an ambition to keep continually the commandments and precepts of the Word of God. They are so helpful, real, and precious that he wants to spend his life keeping the Word of God. He is declaring, "I am going to pursue it throughout all of my life." To this is attached the idea of the blessing that grows out of the faithful observance of the law. There is no real faith without a longing for the Word of God, the presence of God, and for the obedience to the will of God. Jesus asked, "Why do you call me Lord and don't do what I tell you to do?" That is an anomaly, a paradox, a contradiction. There must be a divine enablement. We are to be specifically, directly enabled to keep the Word of God all of our lives.

"And I shall walk at liberty . . ." The kind of commitment that longs to be forever obedient to God results in liberty. What did we mean when we committed our lives to Christ? Was it forever? Did we have the sort of experience in which we wanted to obey and serve the Lord the rest of our lives? Can you imagine the Dallas Cowboys or the Washington Redskins taking the field and the quarterback deciding not to enter the game? We can't, can we? Do you know why? Because he signed up to play. All he needs is a chance, and he will play. What did we mean when we signed up on God's team? When we truly commit ourselves and sign up for life, that sets us free. I am not talking about "liberty" that lets us sin without being punished. Rather, I refer to a freedom that results because we have been taught by the Spirit of God to love the law of God and the Word of God, and we are no longer conscious of acting under constraint. We don't do it because we have to, but because we want to.

Many people are legalistic in their approach to the things of God. They do this or that because they think they have to, and it is a burden, a discouragement to their spirits. They feel guilty and go through their lives under restraint. The liberty comes when we

sign up for eternity. "I am going to keep the law of God forever."
Then we are free not to do as we please, but free to do as we
ought.

There will be times, even as Christians, when we will want to
do the wrong things. Walking in liberty is not freedom to do as we
please, but freedom to do as we ought to do. There are many
things we do and we don't do simply because God says so. We are
to approach the Word of God with that attitude. We are to be directly enabled to keep the law. There is a consistency as we keep
the law continually. The constraint is one of serving and obeying
God from a sense of *want to rather than have to*. We have the
freedom to do as we ought.

When we genuinely give ourselves eternally to the things of
God, it sets us free. There are some matters we shouldn't have to
decide. We should never have to decide whether or not we are
going to obey the Lord. When we were saved, we signed up. "Yes,
Sir, what are the instructions today?" should be our attitude. We
should not have to decide if we are going to do what we are told to
do. Can you imagine an army where each morning the soldiers
decided if they were going to obey the orders that day? We are so
hung up on individual rights and democratic procedures that we
want to vote on everything. Some things require no vote. God
commands us to win souls. We don't need to vote on that. He
demands that we baptize folks, teach all nations, become all
things to all men, be pure and moral, be faithful and committed to
our families, and band together as a church—and we don't need to
vote on those. We are enabled to obey Him because we ought to
and because in our hearts we have already made that decision. It
frees us when we have already made that decision. Our decision is
to obey God. It takes a lot of pressure off our lives when we know
that is our decision.

If we find ourselves in a situation where we are tempted to do
something we shouldn't do, if we are walking with God, we will
simply remind ourselves that we have already made a prior commitment. That commitment is to the Lord, and we don't have to

decide what to do again. Many of us want to renegotiate our faith every week. The contract with the Lord has only one clause in it, and that is: Everything is His. Our lives, our energies, and our reputation are his. That is the condition of our receiving salvation.

If we walk in liberty, it will be distinctly exhibited, it will be seen. These last three verses reveal a threefold way of our liberty in Christ. First of all, we see that it is service of the tongue. It expresses itself in our speech (v. 46). It exhibits itself in our affections (v. 47). And it speaks about the exhibit of our actions, what we do (v. 48). It speaks of what we say, what we love, and what we do. Those are the ways in which our liberty is expressed and exhibited.

First of all, there is determination: "I will speak of thy testimonies also before kings, and will not be ashamed" (v. 46). Perhaps the psalmist is not actually constructing in his mind an historical moment when he stood before kings. He means he is going to be bold in giving his witness of the testimonies of God, regardless of who hears it. When we have this kind of commitment and have received the liberty described in these verses, then we have boldness to witness about the things of the Lord.

Not only will there be determination, but there will also be delight. "And I will delight myself in thy commandments, which I have loved" (v. 47). It is interesting that the committed Christian is tremendously delighted in the Word of God. The burden of the carnal heart is the delight to the renewed heart. The carnal heart finds it a burden to serve God. It is a difficulty. The renewed heart finds itself delighted. Jesus said, "For my yoke is easy, and my burden is light" (Matt. 11:30). If we find it hard being a Christian, then maybe we haven't signed up, because if we really sign up, it is a joy. When God takes away sinful delights from us, He gives us another delight. "But what things were gain to me, those I counted loss for Christ . . . and do count them but dung, that I may win Christ" (Phil. 3:7-8). When God takes away one delight, He replaces it with another delight. What do we delight in? "Blessed are they which do hunger and thirst after righteousness, for they shall be filled," Jesus said (Matt 5:6). What do we hunger for? Here is the joy of a man who absorbs himself in the Word of God. There is no occupation that could be more delightful to God's child than this.

Then there is demonstration: "My hands also will I lift up unto thy commandments, which I have loved; and I will meditate in thy statutes" (v. 48). What does it mean by lifting up hands? There are several things involved. It is far more than just raising the hands. If we are to understand this phrase, we would need to put the adverb "longingly" in there. For a man stretches forth his hands for what he longs for. He stretches forth his hands for what he desires with all of his heart. It is like a drowning man reaching for a life preserver. He reaches and lifts his hands for that which he desires. He meditates upon what he requires. Lifting up the hands is a gesture indicating readiness to obey. It is accepting a responsibility. It is asserting, "I am ready to do what I have been instructed to do."

The godly man is described as lifting up his hands to fulfill the commands of God. The lifting of hands is an act of surrender to the things of God. It may also be an expression of looking to God for the strength to live up to those demands. We know that God has commanded us to keep His Word, so lifting up the hands indicates that we are relying upon God to give us the strength to live in accordance to His Word.

The key is ". . . which I have loved." Why do we read the Bible and not meditate on it? Because we don't love it. We don't approach the Bible like a hungry man at the table, like a greedy man with his possessions, like a thirsty man with water. When we have made a commitment and walked in liberty, then we love the law of God and the words of God, and we meditate on them.

This portion of Psalm 119 is a challenge for us to set our hearts on the truths of God, with a vigorous delight and a devotion to the Word of God. So much we have received is superficial. How long has it been since we have meditated on what it meant for Jesus Christ to be nailed to the cross and die for us? We sing about it, we talk about it, we know about it. How long has it been since we placed it in our minds and just thought on it? How long has it been since we thought of the awesomeness of God giving His only Son for someone who hated Him? Someone might under extreme conditions be willing to give up his son for someone who loved him, but to give a son for an enemy, someone who hates him, is unthinkable.

How long has it been since we have thought that the principles of God are the only ones that can get us through life? Human principles are greed, selfishness, self-sufficiency, and arrogance. But God gives us principles that will guide us through life in victory and set us free to walk in liberty. How long has it been since our faith has been more than just coming to services? Many of us come to church like we brush our teeth. We know it is good for us. We don't always like it, but we endure it. How long has it been since we realized that worship is not something to look at but something to look through? We become disturbed if someone claps or doesn't clap, if someone raises their hand or doesn't raise their hand. We become agitated if the choir is too loud or too soft. We are looking *at* the telescope instead of looking *through* it. Our worship, our time together, is to draw us near to God. It is to focus on Him, to praise Him. We ought to meditate on those verities. Think on the awesomeness, the magnificence of it. God loves me, someone like me with my weaknesses, with my sinfulness, with all of my flaws. God loves!

When we walk in liberty, it is distinctly exhibited in how we speak, how we feel, and how we act. May God help us to determine that these six promises of these verses will be our pledges, our commitment to God.

7

Staying Sane in an Insane World

Psalm 119:49-56

I. **COURAGE:** vv. 49-50

    1. Hope: v. 49
    2. Help: v. 50

II. **CONFLICT:** vv. 51-52

    1. Arrogance: v. 51
    2. Assurance: v. 52

III. **CONSTERNATION:** v. 53

    1. Abhorrence: v. 53*a*
    2. Anarchy: v. 53*b*

IV. **CONSOLATION:** v. 54-56

    1. Melody: v. 54
    2. Meditation: v. 55
    3. Meekness: v. 56

We are living in a crazy world. Somehow things don't seem to fit; somehow things are happening we cannot reconcile. We can't put the pieces together. How do we keep our sanity when everyone else is losing theirs? How do we make sense out of nonsense? That is a struggle we all face, and the psalmist in this passage is grappling with this very issue.

The first five verses deal with the frustrations he is having in the world. He wants to maintain his hope so he reminds God not to take away the word God gave him that offered him hope. He is clinging desperately to his hope. He is still having difficulties and problems, but God has been his comfort. Proud, wicked people have laughed at him, scorned him, and ridiculed him. As he looks around and sees the world, he sums it up in verse 53: "Horror hath taken hold upon me because of the wicked that forsake thy law."

As we look at the world about us, we sympathize with the psalmist. We sense something of the frustration and struggle in his heart to maintain his balance when all else around him is in imbalance.

This psalm will help us since it deals with this matter of staying sane in an insane world. I believe there are four things the Lord could say to us in these verses. *First of all, to maintain our balance when everyone else has lost theirs, we must have courage.* Verses 49 and 50 speak of the courage that is ours when we have hope and help.

"Remember the word unto thy servant, upon which thou hast caused me to hope" (v. 49). When he speaks of "the word," he is speaking of the Word of the promises of God. God had made specific promises to His people through His Word, and this is a prayer that God will be true to His word, that He will not fail to fulfill His promises to the psalmist. After all, that is what faith is. Faith is built upon the Word of God, upon the integrity and consistency of God. It is erected upon the character of God. It is founded on the premise that God will not allow His Word to return void, that He will never betray or turn away from what He has promised. That word makes our faith valid.

As the psalmist begins to look for meaning in the irrational society about him, the first support he clings to is his hope in the Word of God. Then he speaks of the help God has been in his life. "This is my comfort in my affliction: for thy word hath quickened me" (v. 50). Notice that the comfort comes after the quickening.

He is comforted after he is secure in his relationship with God. To be quickened means to be made alive. Revived is a word we often use with that concept. First there is the reviving, the quickening, the coming alive. Then, when we have come alive in the Lord, we have a comfort amid all our afflictions, our difficulties.

In his affliction, it was the Word that revived him. If we want to have comfort and strength in the midst of every adversity of life, there is only one place to find it. That is in the Word of God. Men's words are helpful, but they cannot give peace. Have you ever tried to help or comfort someone, to speak words of strength and encouragement, and as you spoke, you knew in your heart your words were incapable of doing what needed to be done? Every minister experiences that frustration. Sometimes all we can do is put our arms around someone and cry with them because there is no way to say what is in our hearts; there is no way to verbalize what God would say. I am reminded many times every day that unless God gives us a word, we have no comfort. From His Word, God gave the psalmist strength and comfort in his affliction. The Word revived him.

Secondly, this passage reminds us that the man of God is not exempt from affliction, he is comforted in it. We are going to face disappointment, things that threaten to destroy our peace and our stability. We do not have a choice about that; the only choice we have is *how* will we face those hard knocks. If we face them from within the Lord, standing on His Word, we will find that God will give us the grace, strength, and comfort we need. When we go through the fire, we will not be burned, but we will not go around the fire; we will go through it. We will go through the waters, but we will not drown. The Lord will see us through. If we anchor our hearts and lives in Him, if our hope and our help comes from the Lord, then when we pass through those moments in our lives, there will be strength and comfort.

If we would have peace amid turmoil, sanity in the midst of insanity, we must recognize the reality of conflict. "The proud have had me greatly in derision: yet have I not declined from thy law" (v. 51). The first notice about this conflict is the arrogance of wicked people. Here the psalmist describes the situation where he is attacked, ridiculed, and mocked. Instead of being driven away from God, it drove him to God. Perhaps the hardest knock emotionally for us to handle is ridicule. Disagree with me, stone me, curse me—just don't laugh at me. Don't make fun of me. Don't ridicule me for what I believe, for what I understand. Ridicule, scorn, derision are some of the strongest weapons that Satan has against the believer.

If we take a stand for the Lord, we will have to face ridicule. People will laugh at us. We are being told that if one really believes the Word of God, he is not very well educated, maybe even an intellectual midget. "You don't really have enough sense to understand how things are," some claim, "or you wouldn't believe the Word of God." That even exists in the religious world. Those who believe and stand on the Word of God, and have their faith anchored in Christ, those who still believe in the blood of Jesus, are held up as intellectual inferiors. If you don't believe that, take your Bible to work with you and see what happens!

We are going to have conflict. Whoever tells you that when you commit your life to Christ you will never have conflict, never have problems, is lying to you. You cannot have peace in the middle of turmoil unless you understand what is headed in your direction. We must realize that arrogant, wicked people are going to laugh at us. That is what "peer pressure" is. Peer pressure uses the most effective tool of all—ridicule—to get us to do what they want us to do. "You are chicken." "I dare you."

When the psalmist faced this scorn, it drove him to God. It drove him further into his commitment to the Word of God. There is no exemption from this derision. We are going to experience it. Paul said to Timothy, "All that will live godly in Christ Jesus shall suffer persecution" (2 Tim. 3:12). He had this in mind, because he talked to young Timothy in the same letter about what to do when people "despised his youth," when they put him down. He taught him how to respond to that.

Out of this springs assurance. "I remembered thy judgments of old, O Lord; and have comforted myself" (v. 52). Wicked, angry, arrogant people had laughed at the psalmist. They had told him how dumb he was, how foolish and uneducated he was. He has just been driven further and further into the Word of God. The more they laughed at him, the more he remembered "thy judgments of old." That is history. There is a lot of history in the Bible. It is important because everywhere we read, we view what God has done. What He has done for someone else, we know He can do for us. We read how He met the needs of people and how He provided for them. We stand amazed as we pore over His miracles. When we read those things, a great assurance wells up in our lives. If God was able to feed two million people in the wilderness who had no food and provide enough water for them to survive for all of those years, surely God can take care of us. Nothing will happen to us that God cannot handle.

The assurance comes when we face the reality of the conflict, that arrogant people will cause us to be in conflict, and simply reflect upon what God has done. We have a great God who has done great things. He has promised if we will call on Him, He will show us great and mighty things which we never dreamed (see Jer. 33:3). What a tremendous assurance!

Thirdly, there has to be a sense of consternation. "Horror hath taken hold upon me because of the wicked that forsake thy law" (v. 53). If we are to survive in this insane world, we must learn to be horrified, offended, to have what Jesus demonstrated when he had "righteous indignation." He looked at the world and beheld poverty, injustice, greed, sin, and blasphemy, and it angered Him. If we are to survive in this uncertain world, we must respond in horror to certain deplorable conditions. We must never get used to the world. The church was meant to be in conflict with culture. The church was never meant to settle down and be "at home." The tragedy in America is that we have forgotten how to be "horrified." John speaks (1 John 5:19) of the whole world lying in wickedness. It is a picture of today's world lying in ruins, the image of God effaced, the presence of God departed. He says, "In horror I am consumed." It ought to bother us that we are living in a world where our chance of being victimized by crime is stronger than our chance of having cancer, being divorced, or having an injury or death by fire. One out of four will be a victim of a crime this year.

In 1975 there were only 18,151 inmates in Texas prisons. Today there are over 36,000. It ought to cause us to rise up in horror. We watch television, and there were 33,000 scenes of sex, violence, and profanity on network television last year—more than 2,500 cases of implicit sexual relations. We should rise up and say, "That isn't right!" But we merely pass it off and go our way.

Pornography is a $10-billion business. Pornographers in Los Angeles County made more profit last year than Sears and Roebuck did worldwide. It is unbelievable. Thirty-eight percent of female children will be abused sexually by the time they are thirteen years old. A child is being abused every two minutes in the United States, according to Senator Christopher Dodd. For every one case of child abuse that is reported, nine are not reported. We must learn to have consternation. There has to be a sense that something is terribly wrong with this world, and we are going to do something about it! The Christian has no alternative but to stand against what is wrong. It amazes me that we often debate whether or not we are going to do the right thing. In some matters the majority rule does not count. We are not to be a church that decides by majority vote what we are going to do. We are a church that has a constitution called the Word of God, and what it says we do. We have no alternative. We are going to have to learn to have a consternation about things that should not be in our society.

Remember, our society will not understand that. Christians have been ridiculed in the media because they have boycotted some stores and products in the last few years. Several times there has been cause for boycotts, and each time the news media expressed tremendous distress. Not long ago the state of Florida levied a 5 percent sales tax on advertising, and the major networks and advertising agencies have boycotted the state of Florida. But it's OK if they do it. But when Christians do it, it's considered unthinkable.

Sin is illogical. We try to make sense out of a nonsense world and can't do it. It has no rationale. A man who criticizes you for taking a stand will turn around and do the same thing, but he feels it is different when he does. We must learn to live with that, but we must not allow criticism to frighten us out of expressing our horror over conditions around us. We ought to love the things of God, and it should create a sense of amazement in us when we look at the mercies and grace of God and then see how men have responded to God's goodness. They respond wickedly, which is anarchy. Anarchy is confusion, and that happens on an individual and a corporate basis. We are fragmented. That is the natural result of forsaking the law of God.

One meaning of the word "holiness" is completeness. "All the king's horses and all the king's men could never put Humpty Dumpty together again," but God can! God can take the shattered pieces of our lives and put them together. He can put our heart, our mind, and our spirit back together again. He can rebuild our strength. That is what it means to be saved. I, a fragmented person, become a complete person. And the same result can be multiplied in society.

Anarchy results when we forsake the law of God. A society is simply the sum total of the condition in the hearts of its citizens. The reason for confusion and chaos in our society is confusion and chaos in people's hearts. Our society mirrors us. Look into our own heart. Is there confusion, doubt, despair, formality, apathy? How can we expect our society to be any different? Multiply that millions and millions of times until we create a climate of apathy, indifference, and permissiveness. That well describes where we are today.

To stay sane in an insane world, we must recognize the conflict and express the consternation in our hearts when we see how men have turned away from God.

The last three verses speak of the consolation that comes. These are the happy verses. He has spent the first five verses struggling with the conflict, the consternation, and the need for courage in his life. In these last verses, God offers consolation in three ways.

First, "Thy statues have been my songs in the house of my pilgrimage" (v. 54). *Melody.* All along this journey, God put a song in his heart. He lifts the heart with a stirring song. Every step of the way, when we have Jesus Christ in our hearts and lives, there is a song in our hearts. It is important to note that the "songs [are] in the house of my pilgrimage." We are pilgrims here. We are not at home here. We are strangers on our passage homeward. We have no settled habitation, no permanent dwelling place, no rest here. We are looking for a better country, a better city. Never forget that. The Christian was always meant to live with a sense of his alienation from this world.

The psalmist says, in essence, "While I am passing through this life, in the midst of this crazy world, God puts a song in my heart." Amazing and marvelous is the song God puts in our hearts when we trust Him. It is interesting, too, that obedience to God's law puts a song in our hearts, not a burden on our backs.

"I have remembered thy name, O Lord, in the night, and have kept thy law" (v. 56). How can a man come to live by the law of God and the statute of God? It is easy—in the day he sings the song that God has placed in his heart and at night he thinks about it. He dwells upon it, turns it over in his heart and in his mind. His nights become filled with wonderful thoughts of God, of the Word of God, and the truth of God. He meditates. That is logical. For what gives a song to our lips surely ought to be subject to our thoughts.

The last verse looks at the life passing before the psalmist. He thinks about all the days he has lived and sees that it has been mingled with good and evil, with success and failure, with sorrow and joy. He looks at his life and expresses a deep commitment because he sings, "This [comfort, this peace, this song] I had, because I kept thy precepts" (v. 56). Obedience. That is what meekness is.

Meekness is not weakness. Meekness is harnessed strength. If we want a candid picture of meekness, think of a mighty stallion, in all his strength, being guided by the bridle of the one who has broken him. He is no less a horse, no less strong, but he is now under control. That is what happens when we speak of the meek inheriting the earth. They have brought all their energies and the creativity of the flesh under the control of the Lord Jesus Christ.

The psalmist was saying: "I had all of these things. I was able to maintain my balance when everyone else was losing theirs. I was able to make sense out of nonsense because I kept Thy precepts." Obedience to Him is the way to joy.

In January 1970, on a Sunday morning, a group of men showed up at the Red Bridge Baptist Church. It was a little church, only constituted into a church for four years. Those men were the pulpit committee from First Southern Baptist Church in Del City, Oklahoma. They were a fantastic group of men.

One of those men, Cliff Cranford, was a deacon in the church and a mechanic in a Buick place in Oklahoma City. Later he became the chairman of the deacons. He was a pastor's genuine friend. We went through many crises together, and yet his winsome spirit and his commitment to the Lord were almost unbelievable. Whatever you needed, he would give you. He always loved his church. Two years ago, Cliff and his wife Helen moved to Arlington, Texas. He was the shop foreman at Vandergriff Buick. The last time I was with him, I went in to get my car. He had someone chewing him out, but he had a way of just listening and smiling and taking care of it. And everybody was happy.

Nearly 10 o'clock one night, my phone rang with the message that Cliff had died suddenly with a heart attack. I must confess that it left me rather speechless, because I had just been to the post office at noon that day, and there was an envelope in our box, addressed to First Baptist Church, Euless, from Cliff. In that envelope was a check. He had given his tithe and though he wasn't here when we started our building program, he added 5 percent of his income to that program and another one percent to world missions. I couldn't help but think as the reality of what I was hearing began to soak into me, that is how Cliff Cranford would have done it. On his way to a home they had recently bought for their retirement, the last thing he did was drop a check in the mail for his church. He lived and died with a song in his heart because he could look his Lord in the eye and say, "I have kept Your precepts."

If we want to make sense out of a nonsense world, we must settle it once and for all, and do it God's way. That is the only way to peace. Everything else is an illusion. There is no sense in a nonsense world apart from God.

8

God's Word and God's People

Psalm 119:57-64

I. **CONVICTION:** vv. 57-58

   1. Inheritance: v. 57
   2. Intreaty: v. 58

II. **COMMITMENT:** vv. 59-60

   1. Reflection: v. 59
   2. Response: v. 60

III. **CONTRAST:** vv. 61-62

   1. Robbery: v. 61
   2. Remembrance: v. 62

IV. **COMPANIONS:** vv. 63-64

   1. Worship: v. 63
   2. Wonder: v. 64

The dominant theme in this section is the Word of God in the fellowship of God's people. The psalmist busies himself with the Word among the saints. It reminds us that we rally around the Word of God. It is to be our text, the foundation upon which our fellowship and worship are centered.

Interchangeably, the Word of God refers to the Word as being written and also the Living Word, Jesus Christ. It is difficult to separate Christ from His Word. Because that is true, special honor needs to be given the Word of God amid the fellowship of God's people.

The psalmist probably has suffered persecution and perhaps serious material loss. He refers to being robbed as though the enemies of God had taken from him those things normally associated with security. The dominant note he sounds throughout is: While he may have lost material possessions, he never has lost his joy in the Lord. He never has for one moment turned away from the Word or lessened his attentive fixation upon the truth of God's Word. His difficulties have driven him further into the Word and helped him grasp it more firmly than ever before.

It is reminiscent of the saints recorded in Hebrews 10 who endured joyfully the confiscation of their property. We would normally not be too happy about such. Because it was for the cause of Christ, these saints have rejoiced over the privilege of suffering the loss of their physical belongings. Apparently, the psalmist has faced a similar situation.

He has had physical affliction and material loss, and now he deals with the sufficiency of the Lord.

First is the deep conviction of his heart. "Thou art my portion, O Lord: I have said that I would keep thy words. I entreated thy favour with my whole heart: be merciful unto me according to thy word" (vv. 57-58). *The word "portion" refers to or implies at least a worthwhile inheritance.* The "portion" was normally given to describe ordinary pleasures, but here it is used to describe rest and satisfaction so complete that it leaves nothing to be desired. He had received from the Lord everything to satisfy his heart. He lacked nothing. There was nothing he desired that the presence of God had not fulfilled in his life. That was his portion inherited from the Lord. What he had lost was not nearly as valuable as what he had received in the Lord. He received blessings far more valuable from the Lord than he had lost.

The truth is that many times we find ourselves in a situation where all we have left is the Lord, and we discover that He is more than adequate, more than sufficient, and more than we need.

This is an interesting verse because it shows that relationship comes before obedience. We have the person—then we have the precept. "If a man love me, he will keep my words" (John 14:23a). When we fall in love with Jesus, it is easy to obey him. Our problem is basically that of relationship. It is not that the teachings of Jesus are difficult or that His requirements are hard; it is because we have not encountered the Person sufficiently to make His burden light and His yoke easy. "You are my portion, O Lord"—now I will obey you. Our problem is that we legalistically try to keep certain precepts and commands and then wonder why we don't have happiness and joy. We get it twisted. We are to enter into a personal relationship with the Lord first. Then as He is our portion, we will keep His words. As we love Him, we will keep His commandments.

"I entreated thy favour with my whole heart: be merciful unto me according to thy word" (v. 58). Here is a petition, a prayer. I like the idea of the "whole heart." He is entreating with his whole heart. Serving the Lord involves the totality of our being. It is not just mental assent to this or that as being true. It calls for all our energy, every bit of our intelligence, every shred of our fiber—all that we are. With our whole heart, we are pouring our lives into the things of God. That is the only way to be joyful in our Christian experience. Christianity was meant to be a complete obsession of our lives. It was not meant to be an appendix to our lives, not on the periphery, but meant to be life itself.

When we ask for the mercy of God, we are requesting what He has already promised. That is rather certain ground. God never has to consult with the Trinity before He can do it. He has already promised mercy; He has promised it, "according to thy word," the psalmist sang.

God will never contradict His Word. That is why it is so pivotal for us to put the Word of God in our hearts and minds, to allow it to reveal itself to our lives. He may contradict what we think, what the church says, what spiritual leaders reflect, but He will never contradict His Word. God will always respond according to His Word. Anything He does and any action He takes in this world will be consistent with His Word. It is an impossibility for Him to contradict Himself, and He cannot lie.

The deep conviction of the psalmist's heart is that God is his worthwhile inheritance and his sufficiency, and mercy is the promise of God upon his life. So he makes a commitment.

"I thought on my ways, and turned my feet unto thy testimonies. I made haste, and delayed not to keep thy commandments" (vv. 59-60). *The first step of any commitment is reflection.* "I thought," he writes. Thinking is a stranger to most of us. We want to be entertained; we want someone to think for us and to help us pass the time. We are all caught up in that. We watch television, talk on the telephone, carry on conversations with other people, and make notes all at the same time. We want to be distracted and not have to think. We come to church and devise ways of not listening so we don't have to think.

The psalmist thought on his ways, how he was living. He turned attention to his own life and gave serious thought to what he was doing and thinking. There is an advertisement against drugs today which goes "Just Say No." It has nothing to do with religion. A group of young people gave their testimonies on how they realized what they were doing and how stupid drugs are. Just say no! The truth is, we feel the church gives us a lot of rules and regulations to follow, and if we only thought, we wouldn't do some of the things we do or make some of our foolish mistakes. Before the psalmist made his commitment, he thought on his ways.

Committing our lives to Christ is a course to be carefully considered and then deliberately pursued, but we must think about it.

There are four aspects to the psalmist's obedience. *First was his deliberation.* Then he thought on his ways, the way he was living. The beginning of redemption for the Prodigal Son was when he thought about what he was doing. He was sitting in a hog pen in a far country and realized it made no sense. His father was rich and throwing food away as he was starving to death. He began to think about his condition.

Then the psalmist made a determination. ". . . And turned my feet unto thy testimonies." He changed his direction and his mind and put his attention on the Word of God. He didn't turn to a manmade philosophy or a psychological ideology but to the Word of God. He thought on his ways and turned his feet toward God.

The psalmist had not always loved the Word of God and had not always obeyed it. Then he thought about his ways, and he made a deliberate choice to follow the teachings of God. It was a crisis moment for him.

Notice his response: "I made haste and delayed not to keep thy commandments." Sound convictions sweep away all procrastination. When we really have a commitment, we will do away with excuses and delays. One of the marks of spiritual maturity is when we do the will of God right now! The Prodigal Son said, "I will arise and go to my father" (Luke 15:18). He arose and went home.

Matthew was confronted by Jesus who summoned him, "Follow me." The next verse says, "He rose up and followed Jesus" (Luke 5:27-28). Zaccheus was sitting in a tree, and Jesus informed him, "Zaccheus, make haste and come down, I am going home with you," and the Scripture states, "He made haste and came down" (Luke 19:5-6). That is the kind of response we are to give when God calls us. We ought to hear the Word of God and then respond quickly. "I made haste and did not delay to keep thy commandments." He made it a priority in his life. *His commitment involved reflection* (he thought about his ways), and *his response was to turn his feet to the testimonies of God and to make haste to keep those commandments.*

Verses 61-62 speak of a contrast. First there is robbery. "The bands of the wicked have robbed me: but I have not forgotten thy law." (v. 61). The psalmist had gone through countless trying circumstances. He had been robbed of his possessions, but he would not allow himself to be disturbed by the snares that overwhelmed him. But he didn't bog down thinking of his problems. Rather, he continued to hang onto the treasures of the Word of God with delight. You can almost see the sneers of evil men taunting, "Where is your God now? What are you going to do. Look at all your trouble." The psalmist replied, "Though they robbed me, I am not going to turn loose of the Word of God. I haven't forgotten the law of God."

Anytime we make a commitment to God, it will be tested quickly. Anytime we have a high resolve to obey God, Satan will test us immediately. The psalmist had just made a tremendous commitment, and right away the wicked robbed him, but he still did not forget God's law.

In our worst day, it is ten thousand times brighter than the best day of the wicked. There is no hope in this world apart from Jesus Christ. Sometimes we have discouragement, depression, and sadness, but the worst day we have is better than the best day the unsaved have. There is no rest, no peace apart from Him. We will have our faith and commitment tested; we will be afflicted by evil men, but the psalmist wrote that, when that happened to him, he did not forget God's law.

"At midnight I will rise to give thanks unto thee because of thy righteous judgments" (v. 62). When this was written, people went to bed early. To get up at midnight expressed extraordinary devotion and love. It was not that the psalmist could not sleep, but he chose not to sleep. He was so overwhelmed with his gratefulness for the mercy of God. He wanted time alone with God, and the best time to get away from the distractions of the day was at midnight. How long has it been since we were so full of gratitude to God that we arose in the middle of the night to be alone with Him and thank Him for being so good to us?

We are so preoccupied with our wishes that we often miss what God wants. We are so ungrateful for what He has given us that we seldom stop to thank Him. The "rights" we have are only through

Jesus Christ. Anything He gives us is by His grace and mercy. Our part is to thank, to praise, and to worship God. His commitment was tested, but he didn't forget the law of God. Instead, he rose at midnight to thank God for His righteous judgment. He got up just to thank God. Here is a contrast of the wicked and the catastrophes of life with the gratitude for the grace of God and the goodness of God to us.

He concludes this section by talking of his companion. It is in-interesting how much the Wisdom Literature of the Old Testament, refers to the companions of God's people. "I am a companion of all them that fear thee, and of them that keep thy precepts. The earth, O Lord, is full of thy mercy: teach me thy statutes" (vv. 63-64). *First, he speaks of worship.* The word "fear" in verse 63 has the idea of reverence, awe, and worship. He sings that he is a companion of those who worship God, who hold God in awe. He is stressing that God's people need to be together. Union with God is, in fact, union with God's people. Fellowship with God means to walk in the light, and that naturally results in fellowship with one another. God intended for His people to enjoy companionship with other Christians.

The calls of duty and responsibility of our lives may cause us to be connected in some way with ungodly people, but they must not be the companions of our choice. We are to band together with God's people. "Well, you must get out in the world if you are to be a witness to the world," I hear people remark. We are to be in the world, not of the world. We are not to make the close companions of our lives those who do not love the Lord, who do not share in common our faith in Jesus Christ. If we "run" with a crowd of people, we will assume their characteristics. The truth is, if we confess ourselves to be Christian, we should not shrink from walking in fellowship with Christians. Since they are going to be our companions in our eternal home, they ought to be our brothers and sisters now. The believer ought to prefer the prayer meeting to the ball game, ought to love the worship service where songs are sung, praising God, the Word of God is opened, and the Spirit of God is given liberty to move in our lives. That ought to be the supreme moment of our lives.

The believer should want to be with other believers. If we don't want to be with them, one of two things is wrong. Either we are not saved, or we are out of fellowship with God. If we love God, we will love His people. God was extremely wise in giving us one another. We were not made to be isolated. Loneliness is the most dreaded state in this world. God never intended us to exist in isolation. We were meant for each other. The church was intended to be a haven and a place of rest and refuge, strength and encouragement. It is sad that so many churches are being torn apart. People are fighting, bickering, and fussing. It is tragic that God's people would allow their fellowship to so degenerate that the church becomes a battlefield rather than a haven and a place of fellowship.

We may disagree—and we need the diversity of being different—but we don't have to be angry, disagreeable, and hostile. There is to be a fellowship and a unity. "I am a companion of *all* them that fear thee."

People are known by the company they keep. Acts 4:23, after the disciples had been grueled by the Sanhedrin and told not to preach the gospel again, says, "And being let go, they went to their own company and reported all. . . ." They went back to church and bared their souls to the brethren. They fellowshipped together. And John said, "We know that we have passed from death unto life, because we love the brethren" (1 John 3:14*a*). There is a sense of love, security, and ease in the fellowship. *Companions*. That is where our companionships lie. I feel sorry for the Christians who are more committed on Sunday night to Walt Disney than to the house of God. I feel sad for those who minimize coming to the house of God to worship, and then wonder why their faith goes sour. We belong together. Whenever we get together, something special happens. In Western Christianity we have lost that sense of togetherness. Our lives ought to center around the church and the call of God for our lives. We let so many things come between us and the fellowship.

He concludes with a tremendous sense of wonder: "The earth, O Lord, is full of thy mercy" (v. 64). People who worship nature do not see the mercy of God. They see the creative power of God and the awesome intelligence of God, but who can truly say, "The earth is full of thy mercy"? Only those who know the Lord can see that truth. The scientist may study nature and see flora and fauna and certain factual evidence. But the redeemed person looks at nature and sees the handwriting of God over it all.

Redeemed eyes see the mercy of God everywhere. The atheist looks at the sunset and sees a wonderful work of nature. The Christian looks at it and sees the hand of God. Mercy provided the coat of skins so Adam and Eve would not appear naked before the presence of God. The mercy of God held back God's wrath from the human race when man hammered His Son to the cross. The mercy of God transformed the cross from a symbol of infamy into a symbol of salvation. And it was the mercy of God that has lengthened the day of God's grace 2,000 years. God is not being slow regarding His promised return, Peter wrote. God is just waiting for more people to be saved. And it is God's mercy that has met us thousands of times in our journey through this life.

In the words of the old hymn, "There's a widensss in God's mercy."

9

Finding Good in Adversity

Psalm 119:65-72

I. **CONSISTENCY OF GOD'S WORD:** v. 65

    1. Its intent: v. 65*a*
    2. Its integrity: v. 65*b*

II. **CONCLUSIONS OF GOD'S WORD:** vv. 66-68

    1. Declaration: v. 66
    2. Defiance: v. 67
    3. Demand: v. 68

III. **COMFORT OF GOD'S WORD:** vv. 69-71

    1. Evil Intent: vv. 69*a*,70*a*,71*a*
    2. Everlasting Instruction: vv. 69*b*,70*b*,71*b*,

IV. **COSTLINESS OF GOD'S WORD:** v. 72

    1. Excellence: v. 72*a*
    2. Extravagance: v. 72*b*

"It is good for me that I have been afflicted" (v. 71). This verse is the gist of this ninth section. His is a strange conclusion. The psalmist's life is anything but pleasant. There are many disappointments and discouragements, but as he views it, it is good that he has adversity, that everything is not like he wants it. He is learning to find the good in adversity.

We need to discover this because, sooner or later, we will have adversity, and the psalmist concludes that we can find good even in the midst of adversity. We need to learn this soon because hard times have a way of wearing down the best of us. Adversity tires us out and saps our strength. We need to learn the secret of finding good in the midst of adversity.

The psalmist basically teaches that adversity is good if it draws us closer to God. As we search and feed on the Word of God we will find good in adversity.

First, this passage speaks to us of the consistency of the Word of God. It is consistent first in its intent. "Thou has dealt well with thy servant, O Lord, according unto thy word" (v. 65). Even when things go wrong, all is right. Even when things go wrong, God is still in control. He is still good and still working. The most dramatic example in Scripture is that of Joseph. He was his father's favorite son, the boy with "the coat of many colors." He dreamed of all his brothers and their families worshiping him and bowing down before him. He was the idol of his father, loved and pampered. Then, because his brothers hated him, they captured him, threw him into a pit in the ground, and sold him into slavery. He went from being his father's favorite son to being the object of his own brothers' hostility. He who once was free was now restricted and confined in slavery. He was tempted by his master's wife who tried to seduce him and lure him into disobeying his convictions. But he refused.

You would think if he did right, everything would be all right. Wrong. He was thrown into prison for it. He spent twelve years in prison, but then he emerged from prison and became the prime minister of Egypt and saved the nation from starvation during a deadly famine. When his brothers came from their land of Canaan into Egypt to obtain food, he helped them without revealing who he was. But after he told them who he was, he urged them not to be distressed or angry for selling him there because it was God who sent him there ahead of them to save lives. The brothers meant it for evil, but God meant it for good. *It is a vivid descrip-*

tion of the intent of the Word of God. Whatever God's Word tells us to do is best for us. It may seem strange and not in our best interest, but the intent of the Word of God is the summum bonum.

The psalmist, though he is enduring a tough time, says, "God, You have dealt well with your servant." If we will be true to the Word of God and our commitment to Jesus Christ, regardless of what happens to us, a time will come when we will look back and say, "O, God, you have done well with your servant." God is going to be true to His word in our lives. He is utterly dependable.

It is consistent in its integrity. ". . . According to thy word." Everything God does is consistent with His Word. He is never going to act contrary to His Word, in a way that defiles or contradicts His Word. The integrity of God is impeccable. The consistency of the Word of God is nowhere more clearly seen than in the fact that all of the dealings of God are also consistent with His Word. We can trust Him. He never leads us up a dead-end street. If we want to find good in adversity, then we must understand and accept the consistency of the Word of God.

Secondly, this passage draws some conclusions that the Word of God gives to us. "Teach me good judgment and knowledge: for I have believed thy commandments" (v. 66). *He is declaring that he accepts God's commandments.* When we believe someone, we are ready to listen to them. The psalmist believed God. Thus, he was ready for instruction. The trouble with many of us is that we don't really believe God is God and that He knows best. Satan whispers in our ears that God is holding out on us, trying to cheat us of good things and happy times. We often don't trust God. We don't believe God. Yet, the psalmist makes the declaration that he believes and is ready for instruction.

Then he speaks of his defiance. "Before I was afflicted I went astray: but now have I kept thy word" (v. 67). He makes a confession first. "I went astray." Then he speaks of a conversion: "Before I was afflicted I went astray." After the affliction, a change came about in his life. Then there was a commitment or consecration: ". . . But now I have kept thy word." That is one value of

adversity. It brings us to the end of ourselves—to see the chastening hand of God in our lives. God is chastening when He ushers
things into our lives that we didn't want or expect, when they
come as corrective measures. We need to be reminded that His
chastening is always parental, never punitive. It is always corrective, to help us. The Bible reminds us in Hebrews: "Whom the
Lord loveth, He chasteneth." So, God greets our defiance with
His chastening hand and then brings us to the end of ourselves and
to Himself.

*The conclusions of the Word of God are the declaration, the
defiance, and now the demand.* "Thou art good, and doest good;
teach me thy statutes." He requests teaching from God. We can
rest well in this petition the psalmist makes. Because God is holy,
all of His dealings are holy. Because God is love, everything He
does is in love. Because God is kind, everything He does, He does
with kindness. We can ask of God instruction and not be afraid of
what He is going to do. Notice he says, "You are good, and you do
good." To blame God for the evil that comes into our lives and into
this world is slander against God. It is impossible for God to be
unkind and vengeful. Because He is good, we can demand instruction from God.

Verses 69-70 speak of comfort from the Word of God. *The first
half of each of these verses speaks of the evil intent of those who
oppose God.* No one is much harder to take than people who forge
lies against us, to have one's name smeared, one's character ques-
tioned. Accusations are always page 1; retractions are always page
73. Such is unfair and difficult for us to accept. It is one of Satan's
favorite tricks. He is the proud one. Literally that is the essence of
verse 69: "The proud *one* has forged a lie against me." Satan is
the father of lies, who slanders, attacks, and accuses. It is sad that
he has plenty of people ready to do his work for him. If we spent
as much time praying for folks we criticize, it would be a better
world. To attack the character, to question the motives, to forge a
lie about someone is Satan's work. He is having a field day in
churches across America today.

"Their heart is as fat as grease" (v. 70). Fatness in the Bible does not have a negative connotation. In the Hebrew society, fatness spoke of prosperity, well-being. But "fat as grease" is another thing altogether. "Fat as grease" is a negative description. It means repulsive, even if it looks like it is flourishing. It indicates a miscreant who is vile, sensual, who has resorted to the lust of the flesh, who has degraded humanity and is living life at the lowest possible level. "Fat as grease" refers to sensual bloating, not spiritual blessing.

The enemies of the psalmist have indulged in these lusts. ". . . But I delight in the law of God." He makes a contrast and finds amazing comfort in the Word of God. *Instead of the evil intent of those who are against God there is the everlasting instruction of God.*

Notice the last portion of each of these three verses: ". . . but I will keep thy precepts with my whole heart;" " . . .but I delight in thy law"; "that I might learn thy statutes." The child of God finds good in adversity if he doesn't rebel against it, doesn't become bitter. There is goodness in adversity if we don't turn our hearts against God. When there are lies told about us, we are to keep the precepts of God with our whole heart. If we keep the precepts of God only when things are going well, we have no faith at all. If we love only those who love us, that is nothing to brag about, because Jesus said, "Love your enemies."

While the evil are delighting in the lusts of this world, we are to delight in the law of God. It is good when we are afflicted because we will learn the statutes of God. Any adversity that moves us toward God, to our knees before God, is worthwhile. When an individual is pushed toward God by adversity, he gains deeper insights into the Word of God. Things we have known with our minds, we suddenly understand with our hearts.

Verse 72 is a magnificent conclusion. "The law of thy mouth is better unto me than thousands of gold and silver." Two things are significant in this verse. The first is the word "excellent." The word "better" means "excellent." When we talk about the Word of God, we are thinking of "better than best." We are talking about the highest teaching, the most meaningful instruction, the deepest understanding. *Excellence.* Many good things men can teach us, but only God can teach us excellence. The teachings of God's laws are better than anything the world can give, better than anything we can achieve. The Word is excellent.

When God's Word calls us to commitment, it is not calling us to mediocrity but to that which is best now and even better tomorrow! We can't say that about anything else. Satan puts his best foot forward—then it is downhill from there. What we gain with Jesus is excellent, the best today but marvelously, miraculously, it gets better every day. "Every day with Jesus is sweeter than the day before."

Extravagance also is seen in this verse. More than all the money we can amass, more than all the gold in Fort Knox, more than all the wealth we can imagine, God's Word is more valuable. We cannot put a price on the Word of God, on the teachings of God. God who created us knows what will make us happy, what will give us meaning and purpose in life, and what is best for us, so He gives that which is excellent. *But it is not merely excellent, it is extravagant.* It is better than anything this world has to offer.

It comes down to a matter of priorities. Which world are we living for? Are we living for the world of God or the world of man? Are we living for the world of business or for the world of the Bible? Both are demanding. Both require total commitment if we are to succeed, and few people succeed in both. Few people succeed in both because both demand the very best we can give, and we cannot give our best to two things. Our problem in the Christian movement is that we are trying to get the best of both worlds. We can't do it. Jesus said, in essence, "Choose whom you are going to serve because you cannot serve God and mammon. You cannot serve two masters" (see Matt. 6:24).

The treasure of the Word of God, and the corresponding treasure of our spirit and heart when we understand the instruction of God's eternal truth, is better than all the world's gold and silver. If

He gives us success in this world, we have a weighty responsibility, but we need to give our best, our priority to the things of God. That is how we find good in adversity—by thanking and praising God for it and opening our lives to what He is saying through that adversity.

We find good in adversity when it turns us to the Word of God and with an open heart, we seek to know His Word and His will for our lives. As we bow before Him and commit our lives to Him, there is a blessing far better than mines of gold and silver. It is excellent! It is extravagant!

10

Sound Doctrine and Secure Fellowship

Psalm 119:73-80

I. **CREATIVE ACTIVITY:** vv. 73-75

1. Fashion: v. 73
2. Fear: v. 74
3. Faithfulness: v. 75

II. **COMPASSIONATE ATTITUDE:** vv. 76-77

1. Desire: v. 76
2. Delight: v. 77

III. **CONFIRMED AVOWAL:** vv. 78-80

1. Consistency: v. 78
2. Companionship: v. 79
3. Commitment: v. 80

We cannot overemphasize the truthfulness and accuracy of the Word of God. If we don't have a truthful and accurate Word, we don't have any Word. We need a Word. We have proven to our satisfaction, certainly to history's verification, that apart from adherence to the principles of God's Word and commitment to it, there is no real progress in humanity or in mission activity. The Word is strategic. And this passage emphasizes it with the title.

The letter of the Hebrew alphabet that entitles this section is

"Jod." It is the smallest letter in the Hebrew alphabet. Jesus referred to this letter in Matthew 5:18 when he stated that not one jot or tittle will pass away until all of God's Word is fulfilled. The tittle is equivalent to the apostrophe or some small pronunciation mark. Such is the integrity of the Word of God.

Every book, every chapter, every word, even the smallest letter was put in its place by God and has been kept in its place by God. That ought to give us a tremendous sense of security. If we were flying an airplane and trying to read the instructions on how to land, we would certainly hope that someone who knew all about airplanes wrote the instructions. We are on an assignment far more dangerous than trying to land a plane when we can't fly, and that is trying to live life meaningfully, trying to be fulfilled. It is an impossible task, but we have a manual that tells us how to do it—and will never lead us astray. It will never speak untruth or lead us to an undesirable conclusion. It will always bless us and give us a sense of satisfaction and fulfillment. When we follow the instructions and are submissive to it, it will always put a song in our hearts. Before us is a Word from God that is His manual for our lives. We ought to cherish it and place it in our hearts, rejoicing in its truth. We need to take a stand and affirm that the Bible in its smallest detail is the Word of God.

It is important that we say to the world: "We believe the Word of God in its entirety, or we don't." If we don't the world will not be foolish enough to buy it. This passage emphasizes that pressing necessity. The psalmist talks about being "sound in doctrine." He affirms his commitment to God and His Word. There is a different synonym in every verse for the Word of God. He reminds us of his own personal commitment to the Word of God and reminds us of two truths. *One is the importance of sound doctrine and the other is the importance of secure fellowship.* We need to believe the right things, and we need each other.

Notice first creative activity: "Thy hands have made me and fashioned me: give me understanding that I may learn thy commandments" (v. 73). "Thy hands have made me and fashioned me" means that God supervises every birth. God's creative hands are involved in each and every human life, whether it be a child born in Africa, the Far East or the United States. Every human being enjoys this in common. Every child born to Adam's race has had the touch of God upon his life. Every human born is a person, infinitely precious, handmade, and special in the sight of God. Everyone of us is a unique individual. There are no two blades of grass alike, no two snowflakes alike, and certainly no two human beings alike. We are unique, and God has a sovereign will for our lives. That means God has tailor-made a plan just for us. We are not victims of chance, cast asea at the whim of the winds of circumstance—we are created and guided by the hand of God with a providential plan for every one of our lives.

The dignity of being a human being, the object of the love and creative power of God, is what the psalmist has in mind. We can underline the "me" in each of these verses. It is the message of the Christian church. We can preach to all mankind that God has created humans for Himself, made it possible for a sinful individual to be reconciled to God. Incidentally, we never have to convince people of sin. Only in sophisticated Western countries do we have to talk with men about sin. Everywhere else in the world, we mention sin—failing to be what we ought to be, the idea of rebellion—and the whole world understands that. All have sinned (see Rom. 3:23). God who has created us has made it possible for sinful, rebellious mankind to be redeemed. The whole human race has spent its entire history trying to find out about God. We have never discovered a tribe of people, regardless of how primitive it was, that did not have some form of worship, trying to enlighten themselves about God. We have this message: "God made you, God grieves over your sin and has given His Son to save you, and you can know Him for yourself." What a beautiful message the gospel is!

"Give me understanding, that I may learn thy commandments"

(v. 73*b*). Even though man is created in the image of God, with the special touch of God upon his life, he is incomplete. He is an incomplete fragment unless God gives him the gift of understanding. The psalmist is praying that the same God who infused us with uniqueness and dignity would now give us understanding of His Word.

"They that fear thee will be glad when they see me; because I have hoped in thy word" (v. 74). The key word in this verse is "fear," and it speaks about the psalmist's hope in the Word of God. He is saying that the horizons of his life are bound within the confines of the Word of God. He not only speaks of his love for God's book, and declares his faith in God's Word, but he asserts his hope in God's Word. The unsaved people of this world are hopeless, no matter how sophisticated, how wealthy, how educated, how affluent they are. If they do not know Jesus Christ, they are "done for." They may indulge in wishful thinking, but they are victims of the devil's delusions. They are fantasizing with no future.

But that is not so with God's children. They have a hope, a future. Our hope is based upon the integrity of God, His Word, and His promises. The worst thing death can do to a Christian is to tear down the body. The Word of God declares that to be absent from the body is to be present with the Lord. Even death, so feared by the world around us, becomes a messenger to bring us to God Himself. Our hope is in the Word of God.

Verse 75 speaks of faithfulness. "I know, O Lord, that thy judgments are right, and that thou in faithfulness hast afflicted me." We are being told today that if we live right we will have no problems. That is not Scripture. ". . . In faithfulness thou hast afflicted me." God knows, as a wise parent, that we need affliction. He would not be a wise, perfect God if he withheld it from us. God makes no mistakes. God is so perfect that He can take our mistakes and turn them into good. God knows how to make something out of the messes we make. "All things work together for good to them who love God, to them who are the called according to his purpose" (Rom. 8:28). That can be found nowhere in the world except in the Word of God.

No matter how badly we stumble, how many mistakes we make, how many relationships we mess up, no matter how many times we run counter to God's purposes, if we keep our hearts turned toward God, He is able to bring good out of our lives. Our problem is we want that promise without the requirement. It is a conditional promise. We are to love Him. "To them who love the Lord and are called according to His purpose." We want all the blessings of an omniscient God without the restrictions an omniscient God places just by being Who He is. We don't want God to see, but He cannot fail to see. We don't want Him to go with us on certain occasions, but He cannot fail to be with us. We don't want Him to know certain things, but He cannot fail to know so we have an impossible desire. Sin deludes us into thinking we can fool God. But the psalmist simply says, "God, I know you don't make any mistakes, your judgments are right, and in faithfulness you afflicted me."

It is the same message that Job gave in what many believe to be the first book written in the Old Testament. After all the disasters that befell him and his family he said, "The Lord gives, and the Lord takes away. Blessed be the name of the Lord!" He was saying, "God didn't make any mistakes. I don't understand it. My heart still grieves, but I am going to trust in the Lord." Our commitment is to trust God, who is trustworthy. The faithfulness of the Lord is underscored here in these verses.

In verses 76 and 77, notice a compassionate attitude. "Let, I pray thee, thy merciful kindness be for my comfort, according to thy word unto thy servant. Let thy tender mercies come unto me, that I may live: for thy law is my delight" (vv. 76-77). Verse 76 speaks of his desire. He is suffering in affliction, having problems in fellowship, and his desire is that God would comfort him with His "tender mercies." The Scripture says that God holds a nation guilty for the sins to the third and fourth generation, but He shows mercy to those who love him and keep His commandments. He is harsh in judgment only upon those who don't love Him and don't keep His commandments. He lets the consequences of sin run its course in their lives.

God by nature is merciful, and the psalmist's desire is that God would comfort him. It ought to be a source of sweet comfort just to be reminded that in our affliction, whatever it is, the steadfast love of God is present to protect us and see us through. Here is his desire: "Lord, let your merciful kindness be my comfort."

Then verse 77 speaks of his delight: "Thy law is my delight." Now he speaks of God's tender mercies. In verse 76 he didn't just speak of kindness but *merciful kindness*. Here he doesn't just speak of mercy or even mercies but *tender mercies*. He tries to describe for us what God is like. We have such wrong concepts of God. Sometimes we actually think God tries to figure out how to make our lives miserable. We may feel God is the eternal killjoy; He is always trying to rob us of happiness. The devil tells that lie to young people. "You do what God wants you to do, and you will be fat, old, and single. You obey God, and He will send you off somewhere." Many think of God like that. Something happens, and some blame God. We have the idea God is plotting our demise.

God loves us and wants to help us. God wants to lift our hearts and forgive our sins. He desires to put meaning and purpose into our lives. That is our God.

We will never find hurt, harm, and disappointment in obeying God. Our testimony will be, "The longer I serve, the sweeter it gets." It will be worth it all. Everything we come through is worth it in the light of His presence and His grace. Our testimonies will be of the tender, merciful kindness of God.

Our trouble is that we want to disobey God and expect Him not to chastise us, not to respond. Yes, God is One of mercy and kindness, but He is also One who is consistent with who He is and He can never allow us to rebel without our suffering the consequences. Remember that God forgives us the condemnation of sin, but He nearly always allows us to suffer the consequences of sin. That is a judgment we bring upon ourselves. Many times when we blame God for some of the things that happen, God is merely letting sin run its course. Sin is terrible, a poison that inflicts itself upon every life. Whenever we rebel against the known, revealed Word and will of God for our lives, we sin. When we sin, we die a little bit and that death is infused into our being. It is a tragic thing. The experience of treachery and betrayal that David spoke of in Psalm 55 was directly traceable to his own treachery. He had sown the seeds of the bitter harvest he finally reaped.

The same is true in our lives. God allows us to suffer the consequences of our sins, but He is merciful and kind, longing to see us avoid those sins and thus those consequences. That is why He sent Jesus Christ and why He gave to us a perfect treasure of His revelation to us.

These last three verses are a commitment the psalmist is making. He is confirming his own position with God. "Let the proud be ashamed; for they dealt perversely with me without a cause: but I will meditate in thy precepts. Let those that fear thee turn unto me, and those that have known thy testimonies. Let my heart be sound in thy statutes; that I be not ashamed" (vv. 78-80). Verse 78 describes a consistency of his life. There are two types of persons in this verse. One who is ruled by pride, and the other, by God's precepts. One has an inflated idea of his own importance. That is the proud man. The other has an informed idea of God's importance. He has things in perspective. He knows the truth and consistently gives himself to that.

Verse 78 uncovers an interesting thought. The proud are apparently plotting to destroy the psalmist. How often such people try to make men like the psalmist to fail. The devil's people would give anything to make us stumble in our walk with Christ. They will work at it. They will try their best to get us to compromise, to say a word we shouldn't, to criticize, and to stumble. Those are the proud. "Let the proud be ashamed." Their cause is to see the godly stumble, but God is not going to let that occur if we stay close and walk with Him. God's people know that time is on their side. The Scripture says, "Pride goeth before destruction." In time the proud will fall, but in the meantime, they often try to get us to stumble.

Verse 79 speaks of companionship. It ties in with verse 74. "Let those that fear thee turn unto me" (v. 78). For some reason, the psalmist felt that God's people were avoiding him. Two times in this section he said, "If they feared You they would be glad when they see me; if they feared You they would turn to me." It is apparent the psalmist is undergoing a degree of ostracism. At this point we have the greatest testing of the Christian faith. Is the church, as some argue, just a bunch of cliques? Is it really a bunch of groups who like to do their "thing" while the new person and the hurting person are shut out? Is it a place where people can come with their hurts and their pain, and find someone cares about them? Or is it a place where we are so busy doing what we want that we don't reach out?

We can never remind ourselves enough that we must never turn away from the person who has come into our fellowship. Everyone who comes has hurts and needs, and we must not turn away from them. All of us need companionship. The New Testament tells about the Apostle Paul when he was in prison. It was dangerous to befriend him, and many pulled away. One of the brightest witnesses in the New Testament is that faithful group which kept coming and staying with him. Today, in Iron Curtain countries and in societies such as Muslim cultures, when persons are saved, they fall into disfavor with the community. That is why God gave us one another. We need one another. None of us are strong enough to survive alone. The Western dream is the virility of youth, the strength and activity of the young. That is the god of the Western World. Regardless of how strong we become, we cannot make it alone.

The psalmist cries out for companionship. "Let those that fear thee turn to me" (v. 79). He asks that people who claim they love God and believe His Word just receive him. Is that too much to ask? Do not turn away. If there is anything the church ought to agonize over, it is the propensity we all have to be exclusive in our relationships within the church. It is not only a shame—it is a tragedy.

We have to work at not being careless. The purpose of the church is not simply to feel secure in the fellowship with people we know and have always known. The reason most churches in America are not growing is that they don't want to grow. It is unnerving and uncomfortable to grow. When you grow, you may have deacons you have never met. People start making announcements, and you don't know them. "Strange" people start taking responsibilities that always belonged in the Jones family. Growing is difficult, but that is what God intends. He wants people to be brought into the family. He wants a church that will be flexible and loving, and we have to work at it. We cannot rest on our laurels.

"Let my heart be sound in thy statutes; that I be not ashamed" (v. 80). It is possible to be sound in doctrine and miss the mark altogether. Theology is not all that mysterious. God is not irrational. Anyone who knows how to apply any semblance of truth to words can tell you what the theology of the Bible is. He doesn't have to be a Christian. He may not understand the mystery of the Incarnation or the joy of the doctrine of the Trinity. He may not understand those verities that are incomprehensible, but a person who is not even saved can figure out basic theology. He will approach the Bible as any other book, one that means what it says, and the words are genuine and the authors are men of integrity. That is the assumption we must make if we are to study the character of any document. Were the people who wrote it men of integrity? Do the words they use mean what normal words mean? It is entirely possible for a person to be sound doctrinally or theologically and be wrong spiritually. Notice he says, "Let my *heart* be sound." He didn't say, "Let my *head* be sound."

The psalmist is anxious to get right with God. We all know to do better than we do. Our problem is not knowledge. Our problem is that our hearts are not right with God. We don't want to do what

God wants us to do. We resist God. The psalmist, after all this
desire for companionship, comes to the end of the psalm, and
writes, "Let my heart be right, so I won't be ashamed." When we
are right doctrinally and wrong in our actions, we are ashamed.
We don't want to be ashamed so this should be our commitment:
"Let my heart be sound in thy statutes."

11

Has God Forgotten Me?

Psalm 119:81-88

I. **DISTORTED CONDITION:** vv. 81-83

    1. Fainting: v. 81
    2. Failing: vv. 82-83

II. **DESPERATE CIRCUMSTANCES:** vv. 84-87

    1. Delay: v. 84
    2. Device: v. 85
    3. Defense: v. 86
    4. Determination: v. 87

III. **DESIRABLE CHANGE:** v. 88

    1. Revival: v. 88*a*
    2. Restoration: v. 88*b*

This particular portion of Psalm 119 is the midnight of the psalm, the darkest section. Everything seems to be so bleak and discouraging. We have the picture of the psalmist, under tremendous pressure and persecution, pouring his heart out to God. It seems not to matter how much of the Bible he reads, he cannot get an answer. No matter how much he prays, God doesn't hear. It seems as though God has forgotten his name and that he exists. The psalmist feels God has just left him alone and surely has forgotten about him.

We have all had that kind of experience—where we have looked for answers and found none, where we have searched for solutions and found none, hoped for comfort, and there was none, tried to gather some solace, some direction, and it just was not there. If we were honest we would have to say, "God has forgotten all about me."

That is where the psalmist is, in a time of discouraging, depressing, and disappointing circumstances. The writer of this psalm is anonymous. We assume that David wrote most of the psalms, but this particular psalm has no specific identification as to the author. That is good news. That means we can put our name on it. Any beleaguered saint at any point in history can say, "That is *my* psalm." We don't know who wrote it originally, but we know who is in the process of experiencing it—we are. We are walking through it. It is our psalm, our word. We are reaching out to God in the midst of distressing circumstances.

The psalmist paints a bleak picture. He is really up against it. We don't see the light at the end of the tunnel, or the positive side, until we come to the last verse of this section where he says, "Quicken me after thy loving-kindness; so shall I keep the testimony of thy mouth" (v. 88). Then the first verse of the next section, which is perhaps one of the greatest verses in all of the Word of God. It is the sun of God as well as the Son of God breaking through: "Forever, O Lord, thy word is settled in heaven" (v. 89).

These verses have two major divisions and the conclusion that points out the desired change he wants to see in his life. First of all he speaks of a distorted condition. There are two elements of his condition that are really not normal. They are *"fainting"* and *"failing."* "My soul fainteth for thy salvation: but I hope in thy word" (v. 81). His circumstances are trying. He is despairing. He is longing for a work of God in his life. There are various kinds of salvation spoken of in Scripture. There is salvation from sin, from the penalty of sin, the power of sin, to be saved. That is one kind of salvation and, of course, is the predominant kind. It is the greatest salvation offered.

But also in Scripture we find salvation from suffering, salvation from sorrow, salvation from circumstances. It is the last one that this cry deals with. The psalmist is crying for salvation from his current situation. We do not know what the situation is, but it doesn't matter. He is moaning, "God, help!"

". . . but I hope in thy word." He is singing, "Everything looks dark here, but I have something bigger than my circumstances." We all have flown in threatening weather. The clouds are dark and swirling. But every time, the sun has still been in the sky. It is an unforgettable experience to break through the clouds and see the sapphire blue of the sky and the brilliance of the sun. The situation didn't look too good on the ground, but when we broke through the clouds, there was the sun, still there. The psalmist's circumstances are desperate. He is fainting for God's salvation, but he hopes in God's Word. The circumstances of life may seem dark to us—indeed, they may be dark. But God's Word is still there, and will always be there!

If we hope without a word or a promise, we have no hope. If we dropped an anchor, and the rope wasn't long enough to hit the bottom, we couldn't anchor. The boat would still be swept along in the current. For an anchor to work, it must hold onto something. It has to tie into the foundation under the sea. If our hope doesn't have something to anchor to, it is merely wishful thinking. It is not hope. When the psalmist said he had hope, it was based on God's Word.

What we discover in this psalm is: If our hope is in anything other than the Word of God, we have no hope. If it is in our finances, we have no hope. If our hope is in our health, we have no hope. If we are hoping in our own ingenuity, our own intelligence, our own creativity, we have no hope. If we are secure in our home and our relationships, and our hope is there, we are desperate people. We have no hope.

The psalmist writes that his hope is in the Word of God. The only "sure thing" we have is the Word of God. It is the only thing worth holding onto and worth standing on. It alone gives us a basis to face life. Here the psalmist is fainting, longing for a work of God. He longs to see God's salvation.

"Mine eyes fail for thy word, saying, When wilt thou comfort me? For I am become like a bottle in the smoke: yet do I not forget thy statutes" (v. 82-83). Literally that means he has read the Word so long he cannot read anymore, and it didn't help. "Bottle in the smoke" is a picture of an old wineskin that has become cracked from smoke and unable to contain the liquid it was intended to hold. In addition, it stinks. It begins to smell like the smoke. If it does still hold wine, it is so old and smoke-filled that when wine is poured in it, it tastes like smoke. The psalmist is comparing himself to the old wineskin. It is a dramatic statement he makes.

We have all read the Word of God, and at times it did not seem to make sense to us. Sometimes we have read it and gotten nothing out of it. The good news is it is like brushing your teeth. It is doing good whether or not you know it. We don't have to understand it or "get anything out of it" to be blessed by it. The psalmist says he has read until he is bleary eyed and it is of no use like the dried-up water bottle. But notice: ". . . yet do I not forget thy statutes" (v. 83b). The trouble with most of us is that when we fall into that situation, in a dry spell where nothing seems to work, we despair. But the psalmist doesn't forget God's Words. Blessed are the eyes that get strained reading God's words. Blessed are the eyes that are looking for the Lord. We want a quick fix. "Lord, I need some money, quick!" When the Lord doesn't give it, we think He is not listening. When what we fear happens, we think God has forgotten about us. We want what we want *now!*

The psalmist longs for a word from God, but he doesn't forget the statutes of God. He seeks no help except that which comes from God, and he understands that if it didn't come from Him, it would never come at all. The sooner we learn that, the better off we will be. Our only source of help is God.

The Word of God has the power to cleanse us. Sometimes we feel contaminated by the world. We feel the pollution of the world like the bottle filled with smoke, and we need to be cleansed. The only way to be cleansed deep inside is by the Word of God. The putrefying power of the world is more than met by the cleansing power of the Word. We cannot get out of the world. We must live with godless people. We have to rub shoulders with the profane, to listen to vulgar language, to frivolous, blasphemous jokes and smut. We have to live in a world that disregards God, and sometimes we feel dingy and dirty. Like the psalmist we feel that even God cannot use us anymore. But when we feel dirty and useless, God can use us. He can cleanse us. He is the one who takes a life stained, spotted, and soiled, and through His Word can cleanse deep within. He alone can do that. It is good news! He takes our mistakes, our rebellion, and our sin; then cleanses us and gives us His Word. There is power in the Word of God.

When we have failed in doing right and in our walk with God, He and His Word are still there. "I will not forget thy statutes." The lesson for us is that whatever our circumstances, whatever happens, however dirty and unuseful we may feel, we still have the Word of God to cling to. Our comfort and our strength are not in our abilities, not in our reputations, but in the indisputable, eternal Word of God. There is the answer to his fainting and his failing.

Verse 84 doesn't get any better. He now starts to talk about his desperate circumstances: "How many are the days of thy servant? when wilt thou execute judgment on them that persecute me?" (v. 84). Let me put that in our language: "Lord, I know you are going to do something, but am I going to live long enough? I know everything works out right, but am I going to survive to see it?" That is a good question. We know the Lord is coming back again to set up His kingdom, but is He going to do what we need Him to do before we die? That is what the psalmist is asking. These are desperate circumstances for the psalmist, and in verse 85 he deals with the time when God delays. What do we do when God doesn't respond, when God delays His provision, when time is running out?

The psalmist doesn't understand why God doesn't do what he wants Him to do. The only answer to the delays of God, to the silence of God, to the seeming indifference of God is the Word of God. That is all. I cannot explain the silence of God or the mysterious, apparent apathy of God. I do not understand, but apart from the Word of God, there is no answer at all. Philosophy crashes upon the rocks of logic. Psychology crashes upon the rocks of emotion. Science destructs on the shoals of its own presupposition. Religion self-destructs on the shores of its own presumption. The only answer is in the Word of God, and the psalmist said, "I am going to keep my eyes on You." The psalmist describes the desperate circumstance when God delays answering his prayer.

The Word of God gives us some answers that help us in our understanding. For instance, when we read Job, Jeremiah, Jonah, or even the words of Jesus Himself we find faithful men with life falling in around them. Reading these stories to completion, we find what God had in mind. In each case and in our case, God is working out His plan, even though it is not readily apparent to us what it is. God's Word says, ". . . So are my ways higher than your ways, and my thoughts than your thoughts" (Isa. 55:9). When the disciples asked Jesus "why," He said, "What I do thou knowest not now; but thou shalt know hereafter" (John 13:7).

We do not view things from God's vantage point. When God delays, we perceive only the now, only the immediate darkness of the present circumstance. We do not have the broader perspective. We desperately need to have the ability to see from God's perspective. But we cannot, so what do we do? We must trust the Word of God. That is all we can do. God is not impressed when everything goes our way, and we trust Him. But it pleases Him, it blesses God when we cry with Job, "The Lord gives and the Lord takes away, blessed be the name of the Lord."

We must have commitment to God to draw on the strength He has available. We want God's response to us immediately. We want Him to be a good-luck charm to get anything we want. We want that, and we are being told we can have precisely that. God's

Word does not teach that. God's Word, rather, describes desperate circumstances that seem to be unfair and unjust and God's people standing to say, "If nothing changes, I will trust in You."

"The proud have digged pits for me, which are not after thy law" (v. 85). Apparently the people who have plotted against the psalmist have been those who know the law, have abused the law, or misused the law. The phrase "digged pits for me" means they have acted in a lie, done deceitfully. God wants us to understand that He doesn't set traps for us. Remember that James said that God doesn't tempt anyone with evil. That is Satan's device, and it is a sad time when God's people enter into digging pits for Satan. These men knew the law, but they were using it as a tool against him. In our day, there are many people using the Word of God as a snare, twisting it and using it as a trap with which to "get" people. That was happening to the psalmist.

We must be aware of how we dig pits for other people. We do it sometimes by our attitude, by our compromise. Romans puts it like this: "If eating meat causes my brother to be offended, then I won't eat meat" (see Rom. 14). We ought never create a snare for a brother. That is why standards for the Christian need to be held high. That is why holiness and righteous living ought to be the hallmark of God's people. We have such "cheap grace" in our society today that basically we say, "Live any way you want to, do anything you want to, and God will forgive you." Cheap grace means no grace at all. People miss God altogether because we don't hold high the standard. Men use the law, the Word of God, to create a snare for someone else. Let's pull people out of pits and fill in the pits. Let us be those who restore. "Ye which are spiritual, restore such an one in the spirit of meekness" (Gal. 6:1). We are to restore those who have fallen into a pit.

What is the psalmist's defense? "All your commandments are faithful: they persecute me wrongfully; help thou me" (v. 86). *Very simply, his defense is God.* There are two facts to notice about his prayer in this verse. First of all, it is very simple. He prays simply, "Help me." A man in desperate condition does not make a speech. If we were drowning, we wouldn't make a speech to those on the shore—we would just yell for help. God doesn't hear us because we are eloquent. We don't even have to speak any words. We only need for our heart to cry "help." That is all. It is not a complicated request he makes. He is a desperate man, and the clouds are rolling in upon him. He is disillusioned and disappointed, and he cries out, "Help me!" It is very specific, for he says, "Help Thou me." It is as if he has come to understand that if God doesn't do it, no one will. He wants help, and he wants God to help him. His defense is God.

When we reach the point where we are desperate enough simply to cry out for help, help is on the way. Our trouble is we want God, plus something else, plus some kind of emotion, plus some kind of gift, plus some kind of ordinance, plus some kind of understanding, plus some kind of feeling. When we become desperate enough to say, "God, I don't care what it is—just help me," help is on the way.

"They had almost consumed me upon earth, but I forsook not thy precepts" (v. 87). Two words stand out in that verse. The first is "almost." Almost can be a tragic word. If we "almost" get saved, that is tragic because almost is not enough. King Agrippa admitted to Paul, "Almost you persuade me . . ." (Acts 26:28). It was a tragic "almost" because it means he hadn't been saved. It is tragic for anyone almost to be saved, to come close but not be saved. But this "almost" here is wonderful. He "almost" was consumed. He "almost" self-destructed. He "almost" destroyed everything in his life. He "almost" stayed in the pit. The enemy wanted him to stumble and fall into the pit, to deny God, to turn away from God. *Almost* he did but not quite. Almost—but he forsook not God's precepts. He didn't waver in his faith.

God is looking for some people who, though the circumstances may seem dark and dismal and the future bleak, will affirm, "Regardless of what happens, I will not forsake God." If we trust God only when we can see the sun, then we will soon stop trusting God. If we trust God only when everything goes our way, then we have no trust. If we seek the help of God only when we have the feeling and the emotion that makes us want to have God in our lives, we will never have Him. If in the darkness of the midnight hour, in the storm when it seems that heaven does not respond, we say, "They almost consumed me, but I will not forsake God," then we find God. That is God's expectation.

If we make that kind of commitment, we will have this desirable change the psalmist is talking about: "Quicken me after thy loving-kindness; so shall I keep the testimony of thy mouth" (v. 88). Here is what God wants: "Lord, I am like a bottle in the smoke; I am almost consumed. Quicken me, make me alive." He needed life. He had the law, but he needed life. And once he had life, he needed love. "Give me life according to your loving kindness."

There are three steps in this last verse. First there is the law, the Word. We all have the Word of God. What we need along with the Word of God is life, coming alive. Knowing the Word of God, serving God is not mechanical, robot-type service. Once we have life, we need love. That is the desirable change the psalmist makes. "Revive me, restore me."

All of us have known the darkness, what it is like to feel dirty and dingy. We also understand what it is like to pray and have nothing happen; to read the Bible and not understand; to attend church and feel like we have wasted our time. We are all in the same boat. We have all had those experiences.

The good news is that God's faithfulness doesn't depend on whether or not we feel He has answered our prayer. His faithfulness does not depend on whether or not we "get a feeling" when we go to church, whether we have understanding of His Word. God's faithfulness is anchored in His character. If we will commit ourselves to Him, though there may be periods where we don't understand, when we feel like God has forgotten us, God will honor us and someday we will break through the clouds. And guess what. The sun is still there. The sky is still azure. Circumstances may seem threatening now, but our hope is in God!

12
Forever ... Settled!

Psalm 119:89-96

I. **THE PERSISTENCE OF GOD'S WORD:** vv. 89-91

   1. A Simple Declaration: v. 89
   2. A Strong Demonstration: vv. 90-91

II. **THE PRESERVATION OF GOD'S WORD:** v. 92

III. **THE POTENCY OF GOD'S WORD:** vv. 93-95

   1. Revived: v. 93
   2. Restored: v. 94
   3. Restrained: v. 95

IV. **THE PERFECTION OF GOD'S WORD:** v. 96

   1. The Broadest View of Reality: v. 96
   2. The Beautiful Vista of Resting: v. 96

"For ever, O Lord, thy word is settled in heaven" (v. 89).

Think about that. Forever! Settled! We know nothing else forever; we know nothing settled. But forever the Word of God is settled in heaven. That is the most marvelous description you could possibly imagine. It speaks of confidence and security. In essence, God is saying, "You can count on it." Our world desperately needs something it can know for sure, that it can count on. People around the world are looking for the peace, joy, and meaning to life that only God can give.

We found it true when we were in China. We would ask people to look at their lives and examine them in the light of the Word of God. We would tell them about Jesus and His plan of salvation. Some had never before heard that message. We would describe a life without Jesus—without meaning and purpose and with emptiness, fear, and despair. We would describe a life with Jesus as one filled with joy and purpose. Without exception, the Chinese would know their lives were empty and filled with despair. They would want something they could count on, that would be lasting. That is the constant cry of the human heart. God gives this marvelous declaration: "Forever, O Lord, thy word is settled in heaven."

We look at our own lives. We are growing old. Death claims our loved ones. Our own bodies begin to decay. We become aware of our own mortality, our own humanity. We begin to wonder, "Is there more than this?" For many people, life is "much ado about nothing." People live and die, and no one seems to care. But in the depths of our hearts, there is a longing for that which is real, meaningful, and permanent.

This passage plainly states that the Word of God is settled forever. The Word of God leads us to salvation. That is why our salvation is eternal, because God through His Word produces it. It produces permanence in our lives.

In verses 89 to 91 we behold the persistence of the Word of God. It speaks of the longevity of the Word of God. In verse 92 the preservation or the protection of the Word of God is described. Verses 93 to 95 speak of the power or the potency of the Word of God and verse 96 speaks of the perfection of the Word of God. It is a magnificent description of the Word of God for us and its application for our lives.

God's Word is persistent and permanent. It has perpetuity because it is God's Word. That is why God does not need to change His mind. He knows everything. He is omniscient. He knows everything in the past, everything going on right now, great or small, and everything in the future. If God ever were surprised by anything that happened, He would cease to be God. "Known unto

God are all his works from the beginning of the world" (Acts 15:18).

Our passage in Psalms 119 is a statement of the persistence of the Word of God. *It begins with a simple declaration:* "Forever, O Lord, thy word is settled in heaven" (v. 1). When it comes to describing itself, the Word of God does exactly the same as it does with the very concept of God. The Bible never explains God. It never tells you where He came from—it just begins "In the beginning." He is there. He appears. The Bible assumes the presence of God. The same is true of the Word of God. It is settled forever in heaven. He does not give us detail but merely says we can count on the Word of God.

By the Word of God the worlds were established and the whole universe holds together. Paul stated in Colossians (1:17) that by Jesus Christ everything we see "consists" through Him. The word consists means "holds together." He is the Agent of creation, He is the Agent of preservation. He is the Agent of continuation and will see it all through to whatever conclusion is intended in His sovereign will. The Word of God is forever settled in heaven! Whether we accept it or not makes no difference. It is settled. We have heard the expression, "God said it, I believe it, and that settles it." That is not true. *God says it, and that settles it, whether we believe it or not.* God's Word is not so flimsy it depends on our approval for it to be right or on our understanding for it to be true. We may deny it, ignore, or try to get rid of it, but we cannot change it. It is a simple declaration. No matter how clever we may be, we cannot change it, and it is foolish to try. The galaxies may pass away, but God's Word will remain, far beyond the reach of its enemies, forever settled in heaven.

Whatever else that means, it is out of the reach of man. Our minds cannot fully comprehend the Word of God. There will be mysteries in the Word of God that can only be received by faith. It is settled in heaven away from our reach and grasp, but it is none the less settled. I choose to make that declaration. I don't understand it all, but I take my stand to proclaim that the Bible, the

Word of God, is forever settled in heaven. It is infallible, inerrant, and forever the Word of God. Think of those words, "forever settled." We can build our lives on that! It will not change with inflation rates, unemployment, the economy, the international situation. The Word of God is settled forever.

He doesn't stop there. First he gives this simple declaration of the permanence of the Word of God; then he gives a strong demonstration of this truth he has declared: "Thy faithfulness is unto all generations: thou hast established the earth, and it abideth. They continue this day according to thine ordinances: for all are thy servants" (vv. 90-91). The psalmist turns us back to the first page of the Bible and points out that God established the earth. The world we live in demonstrates the permanence and the persistence of the Word of God. It is expressed throughout the world. For instance, on the first day, according to Genesis, God created light, and He set in motion the law of light. The law of light says that light travels at the speed of 186,000 miles per second. Its purpose is to dispel darkness, and its speed is constant. That has never changed. We know that has never changed because not too many years ago a Jewish scientist advanced the human race into the atomic age with a simple equation: $E = mc^2$. That means energy equals mass multiplied by the speed of light, squared. The very "theory of relativity" that thrust us into the atomic age is based on the consistency of a law God established in the very beginning. "You established the world; it abides. They are all your servants." In other words, everything is behaving precisely as God dictated. Everything is carrying out its orders and doing its function the way God designed it. The world is a testimony to the permanence of the Word of God.

On the second day, He separated the waters from the waters and set in motion the forces of evaporation and condensation by which the earth is renewed and replenished. And today that continues. On the third day, He separated the oceans from the continents so we would not have a planet of all dry land or all sea. *He* separated it, and it continues unto today.

On the fourth day, He put in service the sun to rule by day and the moon by night. It became a celestial calendar by which we determine days, weeks, and months. We can go back in history and prescribe to the precise moment when things happened because God put in service for us the celestial calendar of the sun and the moon. It is as if God established it today. It is an evidence, a demonstration.

On the fifth day, He created the fish and the fowl and put the laws of their being into effect. On the sixth day, He created all forms of animal life, and He crowned man to be the monarch over all He had created—and it still exists as it was then. Thus, it has been and thus it continues to be. "Thy Word is forever settled in heaven."

You can count on the Word of God. We try to bend and twist the Word of God to make it fit our purposes. We will always regret doing that because the Word of God is forever settled in heaven.

The laws of light, heat, electricity, sound, magnetism and gravity, chemistry and physics, biology, and mathematics are all established by the Word of God. The psalmist observes that they still remain. They were established and they abide. They continue to this day. Fill a pan full of water and heat it. We would not expect to collect a chunk of ice out of that, would we? Or we take a large rock and hold it over our foot, then drop it, and we don't expect it to fly away, do we? Heat and weight are servants of God and behave like God tells them to behave. It is a testimony of the law. This whole universe is a vivid demonstration of the faithfulness of the Word of God. God will tell us the truth and not lead us astray. We can build our lives upon it. He gives a beautiful witness of the permanence of the Word of God. All creation obeys Him.

Verse 92 speaks of the preservation or the protection of the Word of God. "Unless thy law had been my delights, I should then have perished in mine affliction." In other words, God's Word preserved him, protected him, and helped him keep his sanity. God's Word became for the psalmist an anchor. Were it not for the Word of God, he would have collapsed. He could hang onto it when his world was falling apart. It became a rock upon which he could plant his feet when surrounded by the quicksand of menacing circumstances. It became an anchor that held firm when threatened by the rising gale and jagged rocks. His anchor held firm. He was preserved by the Word of God.

Notice he sang, "Unless thy law had been my delights . . ." The Word of God was no stranger to him. This is where some of us get into trouble. We pay no attention to the Word of God and ignore it. Then we have problems and run to it for help. That is better than nothing, but the best way is to hide the Word of God in one's heart and delight in it. The reason many so-called Christians seem to come apart on the rocks is that they have not delighted in the Word of God. There is our protection and preservation. It will never change and will always guide us through it all. What exciting protection is ours in the Word of God!

Beginning in verse 93 we see the potency or the power of the Word of God. These verses tell us three things. *The first is that it has the power to revive:* "I will never forget thy precepts: for with them thou hast quickened me" (v. 93). *It has the power to restore:* "I am thine, save me; for I have sought thy precepts (v. 94). *And it has the power to restrain:* "The wicked have waited for me to destroy me: but I will consider thy testimonies" (v. 95). The Word of God restrained the wicked from destroying the righteous. Here are three great evidences of the power of the Word of God. How much we need these in our lives!

". . . For with them thou hast quickened me." "Them" refers back to the precepts of God. God's Word breathed new life into him and gave new meaning and new purpose to him. God's Word stored in his memory was used by the Holy Spirit when he reached moments of temptation, decision, trial or tribulation. Then it revived him. How precious is the Word of God! If you are ever in doubt, it says, "I know whom I have believed, and am persuaded that he is able to keep that which I have committed unto him against that day" (2 Tim. 1:12*b*). In a moment of testing, the Word says, "A testing time or a temptation has not laid hold of you with the result that these have you in their grip, except those to which mankind is continually subject. But God is faithful who will not permit you to be tested nor tempted above that with which you are able to cope, but will, along with the testing time or temptation, also make a way out in order that you may be able to bear up under it" (1 Cor. 10:13, *Wuest*). And the Word says, "Count it all joy when ye fall into divers temptations [various testings]" (Jas. 1:2).

In another moment of temptation, God's Word comes to say, "Thou shalt not steal"—in another, "Thou shalt not commit adultery" (Ex. 20:15,14). At the time we are tempted to react in anger and bitterness, God says, "Thou shalt not bear false witness against thy neighbour" (Ex. 20:16), and "Love your enemies, bless them that curse you, do good to them that hate you, and pray for them which despitefully use you, and persecute you" (Matt. 5:44). And when we grow cold in our commitment to the church, the Word of God says, "Not forsaking the assembling of ourselves together, as the manner of some is; but exhorting one another: and so much the more, as ye see the day approaching," and "Bring ye all the tithes into the storehouse, that there may be meat in my house, and prove me now herewith, saith the Lord of hosts . . ." (see Heb. 10:25; Mal. 3:10).

When we are tempted to compromise our lives and our language, the Word of God says, "Let no corrupt communication proceed out of your mouth, but that which is good to the use of edifying . . ." and "Love one another" (1 John 3:11—and many other places), and "Bear ye one another's burdens" (Gal. 6:2), and "Restore such an one in the spirit of meekness" (Gal. 6:1)—and on and on! The Word of God planted in our hearts gives us wonderful revival—quickening, commanding, reviving us. How powerful is the Word of God! Christians never go wrong listening to it and heeding it. The religious mess we are in is because we have done it "our way." If we had done it God's way, it would be different. The reason we have so many conflicting idealogies, personalities, institutions, and organizations is because we want to do it "our way." The Word of God has the power to draw us to God's heart. Thank Him for the power of the Word of God!

In verse 94 is the power to restore: "I am thine, save; for I have sought thy precepts." He is already saved because he says, "I belong to you." So as far as his sin is concerned, he is already a child of God. But he is saying, "Lord, I am yours. Restore me." We need the restoring touch of God upon our lives. We have only to look into our own hearts to confirm that. Can you remember when God was more precious to you than He is today, when He blessed and moved in your life? We must be restored to our former zeal, our previous awareness of His presence. In this verse, we have prayer reduced to its basic minimum. Two words, "Help me" or "Save me," are all we need to pray. Prayer does not consist of making speeches to God. It is the soul's urgent cry to God. It is the kind Simon Peter prayed when he began sinking in those waves and yelled, "Lord, help me!" Sometimes we worry that we haven't spoken the right words when we came to give our lives to Christ. Praying is not necessarily words. Sometimes prayer is sobbed out with tears and no words. Here is the bare necessity of praying: "God, save me!" "God, help me!" This is prayer stripped of all excess verbiage, of all empty oratory. It links our urgent need with His glorious provision, my weakness with His strength, my misunderstanding with His wisdom, my anger and bitterness with His love. It ties me with God. Help me! Save me! That is the power of the Word of God. It has the power to restore my life.

"I sought thy precepts." He may have stumbled and made a mistake, but he earnestly wants to please the Lord. He really wants to do what God wants him to do. His motive is right and he wants to have greater freedom to walk in God's ways. Our trouble is we want God to do something in our lives so we can go on with our selfishness, even to answer our prayers so we can continue in our materialism. But the psalmist wants the Lord to save Him because he has sought His principles.

Verse 95 tells us that the Word of God restrains the wicked:

"The wicked have waited for me to destroy me: but I will consider thy testimonies." There are two dramatic statements in this verse. One is the persistence of wickedness. The wicked never give up; they persist. Nothing is more galling to the wicked than the genuine righteousness of a true saint. The evil world cannot stand a godly person, and the wicked will never give up trying to break him down. They will tempt him with immorality, with verbal compromise, with attitudinal compromise, with material gain, you name it. They never give up. The best example is Jesus Himself. It was testified that He went about doing good. He was a just man with no guilt. Yet they stayed after Him until they nailed Him to a cross, thinking somehow they had gotten rid of Him. Evil people will persist.

But notice he says, "They may stay after me, but I will consider Thy testimonies." What we have is the persistence of the wicked on the one hand, and the patience of the saints on the other. Don't give up. Don't turn loose. Give your heart to God and stand upon His Word, safeguarded by the Word. The only defense we have is the Word of God. We are not clever enough to combat evil, to vanquish Satan. Satan, wickedness, and evil will persist, but the Word of God will prevail. That is the testimony we have. The only way to restrain evil in our lives is to plant the Word of God there. How can we expect God to give us strength when we read the *TV Guide* or the newspaper more than we do the Bible? We are often more interested in the words of men than we are the words of God. We will prevail, evil will be restrained, and patience will be built into our lives when we put the Word of God into our hearts.

Then there is the perfection of the Word of God. "I have seen an end of all perfection: but thy commandment is exceeding broad" (v. 96). A more literal translation is, "I have seen a limit to all things, but exceeding broad are your commandments." The average person argues that the Bible is very narrow. *This verse declares just the opposite—the Word of God gives us the broadest view of life and death, of time and eternity.* All human philosophies are finite, limited, and inadequate. They are harmful for they are tainted by sin. Sin clouds the issue, darkens the intellect, narrows the vision, inflates the ego, biases our opinions. The Bible is not narrow; human understanding is, even though we loudly proclaim our broadness. A good example is the popular "theory of evolution." The first premise of Darwin's theory is that it leaves God out of the process. Some claim to believe in God and in evolution. That is a strange paradox because evolution began as a way to explain how the world came into being without God. Darwin did not begin on any factual basis but from pure theory, and his first premise is that there is no God. Now, how did we get here? That is evolution's biggest weakness.

Then it tries to explain the universe in material and mechanistic terms, speaking of giant forces impersonally and impartially working, following "inevitable laws" over eons of time. It enlists the thinking and the support of the academic community, and un-thinking masses of people acquiesce to its theory. But when we take the theory of evolution and apply it to human life, we have "the survival of the fittest." The stepchildren of evolution are Naziism, Communism, humanism, abortion, infanticide, eutha-nasia, etc. When we apply evolution to life, it is very narrow. It offers no hope beyond the grave, no comfort to the weak. Indeed, its answer to the weak is "kill them." It gives no solution to the sick, no hope for the handicapped. It offers no expectation for the maimed. It gives no hope for the dying and no word to the lost.

Man's philosophy is very narrow because it has left out one vast portion of life, and that is the eternal, the unseen, the spiritual, the supernatural. Only the Bible includes all of that. Only the Bible gives a true view of origins. It presents the absolute truth about God, about the Lord Jesus Christ, about sin and salvation. *In God's Word we have the beautiful vista of resting in God's prom-ises and provisions*. Only the Bible gives us a hope for comfort when we stand at the grave of a loved one, hope to a lost person who faces the uncertainty of eternity. Only the Bible gives the broad view. Man's philosophy is very narrow and leaves it all out. We spend our times chasing rainbows. We grasp the things of this world and grow old, and nothing satisfies. We reach the end of life in hopeless despair unless we have the broad view of the Word of God.

The psalmist says, "I have seen a limit of all things. But Your Word covers it all." All human philosophies are narrow. They leave out God and in the end have to be discarded because they are inadequate. But the Bible gives us a totally adequate view of life and death, time and eternity. It gives us strength for living, grace for dying, and hope for eternity. It speaks of life everlasting in a dimension beyond imagination and of a duration that never ends. When we have said that, there is nothing more to say. All things apart from God and His Word are temporal and narrow.

"But Thy commandment is exceeding broad." What scope we have in the Word of God. It is without parallel, without compare!

13

When the Christian Goes to School

Psalm 119:97-104

I. **SCHOLASTIC EXCELLENCE:** vv. 97-100

　　1. Concentration: v. 97
　　2. Confirmation: vv. 98-100

II. **SIGNIFICANT EXPRESSION:** vv. 101-104

　　1. Purity: v. 101
　　2. Persistence: v. 102
　　3. Preference: v. 103
　　4. Perception: v. 104

In this passage, we explore words that describe scholarship. The psalmist talks about "being made wiser" (v. 98) and "having more understanding than all my teachers" (v. 99). He doesn't say he has *more knowledge* than his teachers but *more understanding*. There are many reasons for that. A teacher cannot see inside of you. You can understand your heart, your need, and how it applies better than anyone else. These are words that reflect scholarship, learning, understanding.

Verse 100 says, "I understand *more*." The setting is in the context of gaining wisdom and understanding and applying it to our hearts. A great premium is placed on scholarship in our society and around the world. In Taiwan, for instance, the number-one pursuit of the young people is education. In our society, the valedictorian of a high school class is often awarded a full scholarship for their learning.

Put this with the fact that a Christian, by his very nature, is a student. I study more now than I did when I was in school. The word "disciple" itself (and we are all disciples of Jesus Christ when we commit our lives to him) means "learner." A disciple is a student—going to school at the feet of Jesus—and we never graduate from that school. We continually learn, understand, and mature in our understanding. There is a sense in which we are always in school.

This passage of Scripture tells us that, in a world that magnifies scholarship, the greatest learning and wisdom come from the Word of God. In most of our educational institutions, there is not much respect for the Word of God. And yet, the Bible is the source of all true scholarship. The impact of the Bible on the English-speaking world (and the rest of the world as well) will never be surpassed. It has had a phenomenal impact upon the laws of the Western World and upon its culture and mores. It is a vast source of learning and understanding, and that is God's intention. If we knew everything else and did not have a knowledge of the Word of God, we would be most unlearned.

The theme of these verses is excellence. He uses superlative words: "wiser," "more understanding," and the like. These speak of achievement and accomplishment. A Christian student ought to be the best he can possibly be. Young people, college students, seminary students, there is no excuse for intellectual laziness. Do your lessons well. Excel. Don't accept mediocrity. People who are content to be less than their best have never made a lasting impact on this world. Jesus kept asking this question, "In what way does your righteousness exceed the righteousness of the scribes and Pharisees?" In other words, don't be content to be like the religious people of today. You need to excel. Don't be content to be like everybody else, whether you be a student, businessman, or housewife. Look up and be the very best that God created you to be. Excellence is the theme of these verses.

There are two emphases to notice here. The first is "concentration." "O how love I thy law! it is my meditation all the day" (v. 97). The psalmist is concentrating on the Word of God. It is not a casual pursuit for him. His daily Bible reading was not just a couple of verses he "got out of the way so he could get on to more important things." He concentrated on the Word of God, occupied himself daily with it. He sang, "I love the Word." There is so much to love about the Word of God. The structure of it is a mosaic of truth. It is breathtaking as we consider the awesomeness of it. Yet, the common sense of it hits us right where we live. The Word is not afraid to deal with our doubts, our questions, our problems.

The simplicity of it is amazing. Wise men have marveled at the depth and the awesomeness of the Word of God. The intelligentsia of society have studied the sublimity of the truth of the Word of God and cannot fathom it, and yet the smallest child can understand it because it is so simple. For instance, consider the key verse in Luke's Gospel: "The Son of man is come to seek and to save that which is lost" (Luke 19:10). There is not a two-syllable word in that whole sentence. The simplicity of the Word of God!

Notice he says, *How* I love thy law." The word "how" speaks of an excessive amount of love, an exclamation of love. The law is God's law; therefore, we are to love it. We love it for its holiness, and it makes us want to be holy. We love it for its wisdom, and it makes us want to be wise. We love it for its perfection, and it makes us want to be perfect. It calls for the best that is within us. He meditated upon it because he loved it; what happened was wonderful. The more he meditated upon it, the more he loved it.

Notice also he did it "all the day." We are not to suppose that the psalmist did nothing but sit around and read the Bible, but there was never a day that did not find him meditating on, dwelling on, and concentrating on the Word of God. *When we concentrate on the Word of God, confirmation will come to our lives.* That confirmation is described in verses 98-100. "Thou through thy commandments hast made me wiser than mine enemies: for they are ever with me. I have more understanding than all my teachers: for thy testimonies are my meditation. I understand more than the ancients, because I keep thy precepts."When we concentrate on the Word of God, it makes us wise. It gives even more understanding than those who endeavor to impart knowledge to us, than those who are older and have more experience than we have. It confirms itself by making us wise. In this sense, wiser than his enemies, his teachers, and the elders of his day.

Concerning David's life there is an interesting little description, "David behaved himself wisely in all his ways and the Lord was with him" (1 Sam. 18:14). "David behaved himself more wisely than all the servants" (1 Sam. 18:30). God's Word gives us a wisdom that makes us wise. This wisdom is different from knowledge. It is not necessarily facts but practical knowledge. It is being able to bring the Word of God into contact with our need, down to where we live. In the Old Testament, one meaning of the word "wisdom" is the ability to do something. The wisdom that God gives us is the ability to live a godly life to its fullest.

". . . For they are ever with me." The word "they" refers to the commandments, not to the psalmist's enemies. It is true his enemies were also "ever with him," as we are reminded in several places. But the commandments were "ever with him." By his choice they were his companions. Just as a soldier in warfare would never dream of being caught without his weapons, David testified the commandments of God were ever with him. When Jesus was twelve years old, the scholars were "astonished at his wisdom" when he responded to them. He is the classic example of one who has the heart and mind of God with the Word of God planted in his heart. He has the wisdom needed for life.

"I understand more than the ancients." (v. 100). That refers to those who were older in age and experience and deserved greater respect. We must be reminded that old is not necessarily synonymous with wise. I used to think that all elderly people were smart and sweet. But I am learning that if we are going to be smart and sweet when we are old, we need practice before we get there!

Someday we don't suddenly wake up old, smart, and sweet. If we are crotchety when we are young, we will be crotchety when we are old. Wise is not synonymous with old. The Word of God affords better wisdom than experience. We all think that to learn something we have to do it for ourselves and see. That is not what the Bible teaches. In the first chapter of 2 Peter, Peter is describing the Mount of Transfiguration where God spoke and said, "This is my beloved Son, in whom I am well pleased" (v. 17). "This is the voice which came from heaven we heard, when we were with him in the holy mount" (v. 18). That is solid evidence. He heard God the Father and God the Son speak. We would think that would be the best possible way to gain understanding, but look at the next verse: "We have also a more sure word of prophecy" (v. 19). Then he talks about the written Word of God.

The psalmist makes the point that experience is not the best teacher. The Word of God is the best teacher. We do not have to eat garbage to know it is garbage. There is a better way to find it out. We do not have to go through the dregs of life and make all the mistakes, become an alcoholic or addict, be thrown in jail, etc., to find out that sin is wrong. There is a better way to gather knowledge. We are being told that people ought to experience sex before they marry; then they will know if they want to get married. There is a far better way!—see what God says. Experience will not prove true in our lives, but God's Word always will. One man's experience is different from another's. God's Word is always the same. The best avenue to knowledge is through the Word of God, not through experience.

There are at least four ways that the wisdom, the knowledge we receive through the Word of God, is better than experience. *First is that the Word of God is more exact and more complete.* We cannot have every experience. Our experience is limited. We cannot do some things now we could have done when younger. And many possible experiences either we did not do or did not want to do. To wade into a lake ankle deep is not testing the waters. It is a limited experience. I know what it is like to live in Dallas/Fort

Worth, but I don't know what it is like to live in New York. My experience by virtue of the limitations of physical life is limited. The psalmist was aware of that. We can even know more than the elders do, because we have wisdom from the Word of God.

The Word is more exact. It leaves nothing out. It gives us principles and direction for every relationship. It will tell us everything we want to know. God will use it, plant it in our hearts, and give us the wisdom to make decisions so we can live the kind of lives he expects of us. The understanding gained from the Word is better than experience because it is more exact.

It is also more certain. There are many uncertainties that arise from experience. It creates more doubt and confusion. But the Word is safer. I thank God that the Word saves people from alcohol, narcotics, and all the other sins that destroy life. But I thank Him even more that he saved me when I was five years old before I ever had an opportunity to indulge in those sins. That doesn't diminish the grace that saves us. Praise God for that. But it is far safer. I have no flashbacks, no hallucinations, no regrets because I was protected from them. I learned at an early age to love the Word of God, and I discovered it is the safest approach. We can mess up our lives if we want to. We can experience illicit sex, drugs, deception, and the like, but it is a whole lot safer to hear what God says and abide by it. The truth and understanding God gives us is safer than experience.

The most obvious benefit of all is: It is quicker. We don't have to live to be a hundred years old to know that God will stay with us all the days of our lives. He said He would. It is far quicker for us to accept it. For us to have the kind of experience the elders had, we would have to live a long time and go through plenty. We can gain a quicker view of truth through the Word of God. Real scholastic and practical excellence comes from the Word of God. We cannot overemphasize this fact.

There is a heated controversy about the Word of God now. It is a tragedy we don't have enough sense to realize what we are doing to our witness. The Bible does not lie. It will not lead us in the wrong place. Why do we argue over words? In a letter I received from East Africa, concerning the Muslims on the East Coast, the missionary writes, "Muslims are taught that the Koran is the only inerrant word of God. In fact, the mosques are showing a color videotape of some 'Christian scholars' saying that the Bible contains errors and that the task of theological study is to decide which passages are true and which are put in by fallible men. It ends with a satirical question that the Muslim-produced videotape asked after this brilliant discussion from these Christian scholars. 'Which of these scholars will be the new Son of God for the Christians to straighten out God's Word for them?'" I have been all over the world and met with many of our missionaries. I have not met a missionary yet that will tell you the Bible is not truly, completely the Word of God. They cannot survive otherwise.

Accept the fact that when we violate the precepts and the commandments of the Word of God, we cheat and hurt ourselves. God is not going to lie to us. We will not be the exception to the rule. We will not be the first one to escape unscathed the mistakes of rebellion against God. *Here is the scholastic excellence of the Word of God.*

Charles Haddon Spurgeon says of this passage, "Let us observe two things. First, it is first person. 'O how I love.'" The psalmist does not say everyone ought to love. He says, "O how I love thy law." Spurgeon continues, "Not only is it first person, but notice it is present tense." The psalmist does not say, "O how I *used* to love thy word." Nor does he say, "O how I *will* love thy word." Then Spurgeon, as only Spurgeon can do, waxes eloquent. "Nor did he say, 'When my affairs get settled, when my ship comes in, when my circumstances change, then will I love.' But he said, 'O how I now, myself, love thy law.'" We will never go astray doing what God says.

The last half of this segment forms a significant expression. When we have obeyed the law, when we have meditated on the testimonies of God, and when we have stood upon its foundation, there are four significant expressions. *The first is purity.* "I have

refrained my feet from every evil way, that I might keep thy word"
(v. 101). There is no treasuring up of the holy Word of God unless
we first put away unholiness. If we keep the Word of God, we
must let go of evil. The reason many people find the Christian
experience frustrating, the reason many grow cold and embittered
in their faith is because they tried to keep a holy word in an unholy
life. Make no mistake. Jesus calls us to a pure, holy life.

The word "refrained" means to "keep close at hand so as not to
be led into sin." A better word for "feet" is "affection." "I have
refrained my [affections, my desires] from every evil way." It is
often used like that in Scripture. For instance, in Ecclesiastes, it
says, "Keep thy foot when thou goest to the house of God" (5:1).
In other words, watch your attitude, your affections. What we set
our affections on will soon become what we do. Just as our feet
may carry us where we shouldn't go, our affections will lead us to
do what we shouldn't. We are to refrain, to guard, our affections
so we will remain pure.

We have seen many people who formerly stood for God, who
have preached, who have written books to help those seeking to
grow in the faith, who have pastored churches, and counseled
thousands, fall into flagrant sin. Such tells us that by nature our
affections push us to compromise. By nature we will do what we
shouldn't do. By nature our passions will lead us to sin. The
world understands this. When people talk about "doing what
comes naturally," they know exactly what they mean. By nature
we always go too far and turn the wrong way. We must refrain. To
speak of refraining our affections means we must recognize the
need of restraint and diligence. Even wise, godly leaders often
need to check their lives by the Word of God, so they will keep it
and not become castaways.

That was Paul's meaning when he wrote, "I keep my body under subjection if, after I have preached to others, should myself
become a castaway." None of us reaches the place where we can
live the Christian life in our own strength. If Satan can reach
Christian leaders at the point of compromise and sin, he can touch

hundreds of others. Missionaries, evangelists, deacons, teachers—none are exempt from the need for restraint and diligence. The psalmist had taken specific steps to check his spiritual pulse and to protect himself, and not let his affections run wild. And he refrained so ". . . that I might keep thy word." If we do not refrain our affections, we are not keeping God's Word.

Another expression of excellence when we dwell on the Word of God is persistence. "I have not departed from thy judgments: for thou hast taught me" (v. 102). The psalmist has stayed with it. Perhaps the best example of this principle is Daniel. He "purposed in his heart that he would not defile his body." That was that. End of discussion. Throughout the life of Daniel, at every point of crisis, he did not have to go back and decide if he was going to be obedient to God. He had settled it and doggedly, determinedly stuck with his commitment to God.

Then, notice a preference. "How sweet are thy words unto my taste! yea sweeter than honey to my mouth!" (v. 103). David had heard and fed on the Word of God. He makes no distinction between the Historical Books, Wisdom Literature, or the Prophetic Books. He makes no distinctions between promises and precepts, between doctrines and judgments. It is all God's Word, and all sections are precious to him.

When we feed on the Word of God, it will be sweet. When we bear witness to it, and thus feed others, we find it sweeter still. The more we talk about it, and the more we feed on it, the sweeter it becomes. If we are saved, we will love the Word. We will love to read it, hear it, and obey it. How sweet are the words of God.

Then he concludes with a clear statement of his understanding, his perception. "Through thy precepts I get understanding: therefore I hate every false way" (v. 104). His perception is: If God says, "Stay away from it," he stays away from it. If God says, "Do it," he does it. God's Word is the source and the secret of his life. God calls us to understand that He has given clear instructions about how to live, what to do. He has told us exactly what the purpose of the church is. He has also given clear direction that our responsibility extends to the furthermost reaches of this globe. We are accountable and responsible. We gather together to praise Him and declare His goodness and greatness. We worship together, but that worship has the purpose of sending us out and affecting our homes, our schools, and our businesses. Through our energies, time, and gifts, we reach around the world with the message of Christ. That is excellence. It is found through our love for, our commitment to, and our obedience to the Word of God.

If we place our lives beside the Word of God, it will make all the difference in the world. If we harbor bitterness—if we have been hurt—and put our bitterness next to the Bible, we will hear it advise, "Put away all bitterness, wrath, anger, evil speaking, and slander. It will hurt you." If we confess our bitterness, we don't have to learn by "bitter experience" that such an attitude poisons one's own soul.

If you have a habit you ought to get rid of, you don't have to wait until that habit enslaves you so completely that it destroys your life. You need only to bring it to the Word of God, absorb what it says about it, and turn your life over to Him.

God has already given us the instructions. Don't expect any new revelation. The psalmist exults, "O how I love thy law." It became the symbol of his obedience, the secret of his joy. It can be the same with us.

14

Light for the Dark Road

Psalm 119:105-112

This portion of Psalm 119 begins with one of the most familiar verses in the Word of God, and it magnifies the value of the Word of God. Here one of the synonyms for God's Word is "light." Light dispels darkness, and it reveals and directs. We who are Christians have one great advantage over those who are not Christians. We know where we are going as we journey through life, and we know how to get there because God has told us. Lost people do not have that confidence and that direction. We have the Word of God, the Bible, to show us the way.

The Bible never uses the word "unsaved." It states that they are "lost." If you have ever been lost, you know the experience of not realizing where you are or where you are going. The best description for a person who has never been saved is "lost." They don't know where they're going or how to know they're there when they get there. But we as Christians know where we're going. Jesus told His disciples, though they were certainly bewildered at the moment, "The way I go, you know. I am the way, the truth, and the life. No one comes unto the Father but by me" (see John 14:6). We have great confidence. We are not left by ourselves. We have light for the dark valley, for those days that lie ahead. We have found The Way. We know where we are headed. We are going home. The very worst life can do to me is to take me home! God has given us the precious treasure of His Word to be a light for us on the path that lies ahead.

This passage reveals three things about the light of the Word of God. First of all, it tells us that the Bible is here as light, giving us direction for our lives, a defense, and then delight. *The first three verses tell us that the light points our direction.* "Thy word is a lamp unto my feet, and a light unto my path. I have sworn, and I will perform it, that I will keep thy righteous judgments. I am afflicted very much: quicken me, O Lord, according unto thy word. Accept, I beseech thee, the freewill offerings of my mouth, O Lord, and teach me thy judgments" (vv. 105-108).

The light points our direction for our obedience. If we want to know what to do, God's Word is a lamp unto our feet and a light unto our path. Those two phrases are most descriptive. A light shows us the road; a lamp shows us the next step. We may not have all the details, but we have in God's Word light to reveal the overall direction, and we have a lamp to show us how to make the next step. The Word helps us to make decisions in our lives. Many of us are facing decisions that we must make quickly. It is not left up to us to decide on the basis of how we feel or some kind of intuition. We have a word from God. He will show us from His Word what He wants us to do.

The Bible presents us a great deal of direction. For instance, it tells us that "God is not the author of confusion" (see 1 Cor. 14:33). So confusion is no answer; confusion means no. God doesn't initiate confusion. If you don't know what to do, then your answer is to do nothing. Unless God gives you clear conviction (and this is how it gives us light for the next step), His Word urges us not to act out of doubt. If we do, it is wrong. "Whatsoever is not of faith is sin" (Rom. 14:23*b*). Many of us have tough decisions to make, and our prayer to God is for His Word to be clear to us as we dwell in it.

We must be sure about abiding in His Word. If we reach the point of decision-making and start random flipping through the Bible, hoping to find something, then we are misusing God's Word. The Bible speaks of abiding in the Word of God. It ought to be a habit. If God is going to speak to you, He will speak through His Word during the course of your daily reading and studying.

God's Word can give us direction for every decision we ever have to make. He is referring to how God leads us. He doesn't unroll a whole map where we can see the end of the road and anticipate every turn along the way. It is good that now we do not know every encounter we have to face. Not knowing creates a tremendous opportunity for us to trust God and to praise Him for what He does, step by step. We do know the big picture, and His Word gives us a lamp so we can know the next step to take.

This particular verse, speaking of direction, refers to our obedience. ". . . That I will keep thy righteous judgments" (v. 106). The Word of God gives us light for our obedience. The psalmist pledges to keep the precepts of God, His righteous judgments. This little phrase, "I have sworn and I will perform it," is in the perfect tense. It could be translated, "I *have performed* it." He could be making a statement of his obedience, or he could be saying that he is pledging to keep the Word of God. But it is a strategic statement that we go to the Word of God to find light for our obedience.

Another thought about a light and a lamp is that a light is generally associated with the day, and a lamp, with the night. It is a reminder that God's Word by day and by night guides us through all the experiences of life.

Verse 107 teaches us that light points our direction for our obstacles. "I am afflicted very much: quicken me, O Lord, according unto thy word" (v. 107). He is suffering awful afflictions and depression. Those are not unusual companions. It is common for someone under affliction also to be depressed. The psalmist is, and he lays it before God. The psalmist confronts his affliction, which comes from his enemies—from the outside, and his depression, which comes from the inside—his internal fears, his anxieties. Where is he going to turn? There is only one place—to his Lord to find light for his obstacles.

He prays, ". . . Quicken me." That speaks of his spirit. "Revive me," he means. In other words, he had allowed his circumstances to get him down. The Word of God fortifies one's spirit, heart, and soul, and it revives one's inward being. It deals with anxiety, guilt, depression, fears, everything that tortures us. Whatever the circumstances, tell it to God. If our desire is according to His Word, then He will respond as we have requested. Whatever obstacle is there, the Word of God gives us light in dealing with that obstacle.

The Word is also there to give us light for our offerings. "Accept, I beseech thee, the freewill offerings of my mouth, O Lord, and teach me thy judgments." The greatest—and also the most common—of all the freewill offerings in the Old Testament was the burnt offering, where a slain animal was burned on the altar. But the psalmist here sings, "Lord, I want to ask you to accept the freewill offering of my mouth."

The psalmist understood that worship was more than making sacrifices and keeping rituals. In Psalm 51 the psalmist makes it plain:

> For thou desirest not sacrifice; else would I give it: thou delightest not in burnt offering. The sacrifices of God are a

> broken spirit: a broken and a contrite heart, O God, thou
> wilt not despise (vv. 16-17).

God does not want mechanical conformity or mere ritual from those who worship Him. Apparently, he is speaking of a word of praise. It is the sacrifice of thanksgiving that Hebrews 13:15 speaks of, where we thank and praise God. That is a pleasing sacrifice to God. Just because we come to church and sit in the building, go through the motions, and be quiet while the preacher is talking, doesn't mean we have worshiped. Worship is not going through ritual. Remember when Jesus talked about how people make their offerings. It was not the amount that counted—it was the attitude with which it was given. The poor widow who gave a mite gave everything she had. The amount was insignificant, but what her heart spoke was important. God's Word tells us how to approach God, teaches us how to praise God, and trains us how to give to him the freewill offering of our lips.

The Word of God is also light that presents our defense. "My soul is continually in my hand: yet do I not forget thy law" (v. 109). Literally, he is saying, "My heart is in my throat." He was scared to death. Yet, he did not ". . . forget thy law. The wicked have laid a snare for me: yet I erred not from thy precepts" (v. 110).

First of all, it presents our defense against anxieties. His dangers were real, and he was frightened. But the Word of God gave him confidence that quieted his fears. Notice the word "yet" in verse 109. Many times when we are submerged in the anxieties of life, we forget about God. Many times when we are frightened, we do not have time for God's Word. But the psalmist confessed, "Even though I was frightened to death, even though I was caught in the trap of anxiety, I didn't forget your law." Whenever we feel the most insecure, then we need the Word of God the most. He did not let his circumstances repel him from God.

Then it gives us defense against our adversaries. Verse 110 speaks of the wicked laying snares for him. He was edgy because some were trying to trick him and ensnare him. When we are under attack, it is easy to avoid what God says. After all, we have been attacked, and sometimes our response tends to be revengeful. That is counter to the law of God. We may have a godly cause, but many times we pursue a godly goal in an ungodly manner. The psalmist had adversaries who had laid traps for him. Doubtlessly, they had accused him, misrepresented him, and made slanderous remarks. In spite of that, he did not stray from the law. If only we would follow his example, it would solve so much heartache.

If we are out of sorts with a brother, we are to ask his forgiveness, according to the Bible. Forgive him. Confront him. No, but we don't want to do that. There is sort of a devilish joy in being angry. We often want to respond the way the world does. The psalmist did not react inconsistently with God's Word. Whatever comes, the Word of God must always be followed.

The Word of God is our light to point our direction, to present our defense, and then to provide our delight. A lot can be told about someone by what delights them. "Thy testimonies have I taken as an heritage for ever: for they are the rejoicing of my heart. I have inclined mine heart to perform thy statutes alway, even unto the end" (vv. 111-112). The Word provides our delight in rejoicing. Do we find our great delight there?

The trouble with most of us is that we know just enough Bible to be dangerous. We take it out of context and build systems. That is how cults are formed, heresy is begun. You see, atheism is not a heresy. No one pays much attention to atheism. It is the spinoffs of the Christian faith that are distorted, twisted, perverted. They constitute heresy. That happens when we don't delight ourselves in the Word of God.

The Word of God is light to give us joy. It is the most priceless heritage we have. "Thy testimonies have I taken as an heritage." A heritage is an inheritance. The greatest inheritance in the world is the Word of God—but it requires work. We must give ourselves to it; read it; study it; reflect upon it. Some of us spend more time reading books about the Bible than we do reading the Bible itself.

There are good books, but they can never replace the Word of God in our lives. That is what the priesthood of the believer means. We have a right to go to God ourselves. No preacher has to tell us what is right or wrong. We can go directly to God ourselves. The Bible in common language was the greatest revolution of the last 2,000 years, when people like us could read it. It is supposed to delight us, and it causes rejoicing.

And it causes reflection. "I have inclined mine heart to perform thy statutes alway, even unto the end." When we rejoice in the Word of God and reflect on it, we will be consistent in the way we live it. There is no turning back because we are going to follow the Lord. I remember years ago when I was in a youth revival in Huffman, Texas. It was out in the middle of nowhere. One day, while I was in Huffman, I got on a horse. It looks so easy to ride a horse. Everything went great until I made the mistake of turning the horse toward the barn. All the strength I had, all the "whoas" that were in me, couldn't slow him down. He saw that barn and took off. All I could do was hang on and hope I didn't fall off. He was headed home!

The Christian who dwells in the Word of God is like that old horse when he heads home, and our rejoicing ought to be in what God has given us. It ought to be as much of an intense drive and energetic response as that old horse heading for the barn. We ought to love the Word of God with all of our hearts. The commitment of the psalmist is: "I have inclined my heart to perform your statutes alway, even unto the end." "I am going home, and I am going with Jesus" is the decision we ought to make. Our trouble is, we want to negotiate every decision. We cannot negotiate with God. Jesus has only one condition for discipleship. That is surrender. Give up. If we don't take up our cross daily and deny ourselves, we cannot be His disciple. So, we must accept it. As we head home, He has given us light for the journey.

It is light that points out our direction, presents our defense, provides our delight. Our problem with this light is not that it is obscure. It is not that there are some things we don't understand; it is that we are not willing to do what we know it tells us to do. The psalmist made his choice. He was going home. God had given him light for the journey, and to the end he was going to pursue it. That is superlative advice.

15

Dealing with Peer Pressure

Psalm 119:113-120

I. **HIS CONFLICT:** vv. 113-115

    1. Genuine Pressure: v. 113
    2. Generous Provision: v. 114
    3. Guarded Promise: v. 115

II. **HIS CONCERN:** vv. 116-117

    1. For Consistent Actions: v. 116
    2. For Continual Actions: v. 117

III. **HIS CONCLUSION:** vv. 118-119

    1. The Retribution of God: vv. 118-119
    2. The Reverence of God: v. 120

Each section of this psalm has a unique slant of special value and emphasis for our lives. This one deals with the pressure the psalmist feels from people who don't like him. He calls them "evildoers" and his "enemy." They put pressure on him to do things inconsistent with the Word of God, and this passage deals with his response to them.

He prays that God would deal with them and that he will remain loyal to the Word of God in the midst of all this pressure. He is particularly preoccupied with these evildoers. We do not really hear about "peer pressure" when it comes to doing good. Usually when we think of peer pressure it is to do something bad.

He talks to his peers about God, and then he talks to God about them. Throughout this entire segment of this psalm, he declares his own personal loyalty to the Word of God. In the first few verses he admits he has a real problem with his own heart. Sometimes he is tempted to sin and he has a tendency to respond in wrongful ways. He is admitting honestly what he sees as a weakness in his own life. The Apostle Paul spoke about the same struggle in his own life in Romans 7.

This psalm is for all of us who, at one time or another, struggle in our spiritual walk. The psalmist is in that predicament. *In the first three verses he talks about his conflict.* "I hate vain thoughts: but thy law do I love. Thou art my hiding place and my shield: I hope in thy word. Depart from me, ye evildoers: for I will keep the commandments of my God" (vv. 113-115). First, he says *there is genuine pressure being brought to bear on him.* The phrase "vain thoughts" could be translated "divided thoughts." It means what we would understand as doubleminded, fickle. It means he doesn't always do what he says he will do. He is continually pressured by his foes, and he admits a tendency to vacillate. His battle was really between what he was being pressured to do and his faithfulness to the Word of God. The struggle is between his thoughts and the Word of God. Truthfully, all of us have our moments of doubt. If we would be honest, we would admit there are times when our reasoning comes up with the conclusion that it might not be so bad to compromise. After all, we made our commitment to God in the heat of emotion, or in the fervor of a high spiritual moment. We feel we may have gone "overboard." So, why not let down a little bit?

The psalmist is caught in the midst of his own doubts and his temptation to compromise, and he admits it. The word translated "vain" is found in other places in the Old Testament. Elijah on Mount Carmel asked the people, "How long will ye halt between two opinions?" (1 Ki. 18:21). The word "halt" is from the same root word that we translate "vain" or "divided." It literally means "to leap." That is what a double-minded man does. One who is fickle and vacillates leaps from one thing to another. The psalmist hated that, especially because of his own tendency to do it. We find a man who admits he does not always want to do right. He has divided thoughts. There are times when he is more fervent than at others. He is in conflict.

What does he do? ". . . But thy law do I love." He has been leaping back and forth from one thing to another. He is going to make one final leap and come down squarely on the Word of God. The Word is going to be the arbiter of his conscience, the ruler of his will, the love of his life, the food for his thoughts. He hates what he sees in himself, so he chooses to love the law of God.

He says "I hate" and "I love." This is a most important issue for each of us. Every negative has a positive. It will do no good for us to hate our vacillation, if we don't love something. While the psalmist hates the sins in his life, he loves the Word of God. If we are distressed and upset with the sins we see in ourselves, the only way to get over it is to love the Word of God. Then the Word becomes a balancing influence; once we are balanced by the Word, we become steadfast, unmoveable in the things of the Lord (see 1 Cor. 15:58).

He speaks of the generous provision that has been made for him. "Thou art my hiding place and my shield: I hope in thy word" (v. 114). God has made provision. We need a hiding place when we are threatened by danger, a shield when it is an intimidation. God is the psalmist's hiding place and his shield when danger confronts him. His first line of defense is in the presence of the Lord; his last line of defense is the same. He has no other defense; he needs no other defense. His hope is not in his friends, his family, his own strength and resources, his skill with the sword, and the like, but in God and in His Word. Since God cannot fail to do what He promised, victory is assured. It never enters the psalmist's mind that he won't succeed because he knows God will keep His Word. God must be true to His character.

It bothers some that the psalmist has as much hope in the Word of the Lord as he does in the Lord. That is normal since both loyalties run parallel. We cannot love the Lord if we do not love His Word. We do not hope in the Lord if we do not hope in His Word. Both those loyalties are essential.

In verse 115 he issues a guarded promise: ". . . For I will keep the commandments of my God." He tells his enemies it is no use for them to try to entice him into doing evil. He has made up his mind and is committed to keeping God's Word. It is a good practice to put a great deal of distance between us and those who would tempt us to do evil. The psalmist tells them to "get away." Imagine how different history would be if, when Satan came to Eve and began to talk to her, she had protested, "Get away. I do not want to talk to you." And what if Adam had obeyed the one command God gave him not to eat of the fruit of the tree and had said, "We will not do that. Get away from here"? Eve's first mistake was that she flirted with temptation. She entered into a conversation with Satan. He has nothing good to offer us and will never lead us to do the good. He is the father of evil. He is the enemy, the prince of darkness, the accuser. Get away from him. Before long Eve was negotiating what God had said, and that will happen to us, unless we keep the commandments of God and put distance between us and those who would cause us to sin. Our friends need to be people who love the Lord. It does not mean we have no contact or relationships with other people. Certainly we try to build relationships to witness, but people we allow to put peer pressure on us need to be Christians.

When we come into the New Testament, the conflict is called "spiritual warfare." We are opposed by hostile, evil forces that want to do all they can to cause us to stumble. They will facilitate your doing the wrong things. The psalmist says, "Get away from me. I am going to keep the commandments of the Lord."

In verse 116 he expresses concern that he have consistent actions. "Uphold me according unto thy word, that I may live: and let me not be ashamed of my hope." He understands that the resolve he has just declared would melt fast in the fires of temptation. I know of no Christian who has set out to disobey God and compromise his faith, but we find our good intentions are often diluted in the time of temptation. The psalmist knows he cannot trust himself. The sooner we learn that, the better off we will be. We cannot trust ourselves. Without the guarding, sustaining power of the Holy Spirit in our lives, there is nothing we will not do. We are capable of being immoral, dishonest, deceitful, slanderous, unkind, and hateful.

We need the consistency the psalmist prays for, ". . . according to thy word." God has promised to do just that. Hope built on the promise of God has a claim on God. When we ask God to deal with us according to His Word, He has to respond. God's Word undergirds the psalmist's faith; it stiffens his resolve; it gives him a backbone to live consistently. When there are elements in our lives, when there is peer pressure to do wrong, we need to bathe our souls in the Word of God and put God's Word in our hearts. "Thy word have I hid in mine heart, that I might not sin against thee" (Ps. 119:11). If we want the protection and the shielding power of God's Word, then we must live in it, dwell in it.

In verse 117, he has the desire and concern for continual action. "Hold thou me up, and I shall be safe: and I will have respect unto thy statutes continually." There are two sides to the same coin. He asks that all his actions be consistent. In other words, he asks that he act consistently with how he has acted. When he expresses his faith in God, he wants it to be consistent. But he also says, ". . . let them be continual." It is a prayer for perseverance. He is concerned that his actions be consistent and that they be continual.

Then he draws a conclusion. The last three verses initially deal with the retribution, the judgment of God. "Thou hast trodden down all them that err from thy statutes: for their deceit is falsehood. Thou puttest away all the wicked of the earth like dross: therefore I love thy testimonies" (vv. 118-119). The words "trodden down" mean literally "to set at naught," "to have no effectiveness." That is how God dealt with these people. They had set at nought His Word, so God set them at nought. God set them aside. "Dross," the impurities, in a smelter where metal is purified rises to the top to be skimmed off and thrown away. The psalmist says that is how God has treated evil people who have acted and lived against the Word of God.

It is interesting that he writes these verses in the past tense. Yet, the battle is not over. He is still in the middle of the struggle, yet he says, "Thou hast . . ." The fate of these moral, political, religious, cultural cheaters and pretenders is sealed. The battle is still going on, but they are through. They have no future. God has already judged them. That is the fate of those who disregard the Word of God.

Understanding that God has already won the victory fortifies the psalmist to love God and His Word even more than ever. This is a simple description of how God has acted in history. Sometimes, there will be a sweeping holocaust of judgment such as the Flood or the destruction of Sodom and Gomorrah. He uses famine, war, and pestilence to judge the wicked. God allows the wickedness of a society to be brought to a boil, rise to the surface, and then skims it off. That means God will have to judge us in our society. His judgment will fall on the permissive society of America based on what God has always done in the past. Billy Graham declares that if God does not judge us, He will have to apologize to Sodom and Gomorrah. There is a total disregard for the right, for morality, for integrity, and the rest of God's standards. Judgment is coming. And the psalmist says God has already judged the enemies of righteousness. The battle is really over, and evil is not going to win. We understand that because we have read the Book of Revelation. Satan is doomed. There is already a lake of fire prepared for Satan and his angels. The struggle is still real for us, but there is no doubt about the outcome.

Then he speaks of the reverence of God. "My flesh trembleth for fear of thee; and I am afraid of thy judgments" (v. 120). There is a reverent fear that fills the psalmist's heart as he thinks of the greatness of this God he knows. Literally, that verse reads, "My flesh creeps for fear of thee." Some people describe God as being too kind and too merciful to be a God of judgment. To them, God is some kind of a cosmic Santa Claus. The folks who have a God like that do not know the God of the Bible. He is the God of infinite love. He loves us so totally and infinitely that He Himself, in the person of His Son, paid the price for our sins. He loves with an everlasting love. But there can be no genuine love without the flip side, which is the holiness of God. While He is a God of love, He is a God of holiness, and He must judge sin. He cannot pass it off as being of no consequence. He must judge sin.

The psalmist is afraid of God's judgments. God would never have us become so "familiar" with Him and holy things that we have contempt. We need to realize who God is. He is not some insipid, harmless old man who does not have enough sense to know what is going on. He is a holy God. We act as if He were deaf and blind and dumb. We act as if He does not care what we do, as if He has no idea what we do. Just listen to the prayers we pray. We are always telling Him things. Why do we try to instruct Him? We have treated Him with such disregard and disrespect for His holiness that we do not take Him seriously. God is a holy God, and we must deal with Him on the basis of our understanding of who He is, of a reverence for Him.

When we think of His holiness and His judgment, we get goose bumps. Our flesh crawls with an understanding of who He is and what He does, and that He is a God who can uphold us. He can move in our lives, giving us victory. He loves us and wants us to love Him, but He will never let us forget His holiness and His judgment. To be honest, we are afraid of the judgments of God. We want mercy, not justice. What if God took away all the excuses we use for not serving Him? What if He took away the children parents use as an excuse for not serving God? What if He snatched away all the husbands and wives we use; the honors we use; and the business opportunities men use as an excuse. Thank God, He doesn't. While we deserve that, He treats us with mercy and grace. We must respect a God like that. If He treated us as we deserve, it would be all over. Though we grieve Him, He loves us—but there is a point beyond which His love cannot extend and still be holy, beyond which the mercy of God cannot continue to manifest itself or will cease to be a virtue. God's judgment is a reality.

The only way we can truly love God is to respect and reverence what He has to do in response to evil. We love Him for His mercy and grace, but the only way we can grow stronger is to understand that His mercy and grace came at immeasurable cost. In history, on a real day, Jesus Christ was born as a babe in Bethlehem. With real, human flesh, He grew to maturity. Though He was man, He never sinned. He never spoke a word He shouldn't have, never took a step He shouldn't have, never touched anything He shouldn't have. And on a real day, He was nailed to a cross to die for sins He didn't commit. When God tells us He loves us, we must be aware that His love is so strong that at a point in time, it cost God His Son to love us. It cost Him the death of Jesus Christ to show us mercy, to manifest His grace to us. There will be a point beyond which His grace will not go with us.

For the Christian, it means discipline. For all believers it means the judgment seat (the Bema) of Christ. The day is coming when we stand to give an account. For those who have never received Christ, there wil come a day of judgment at the Great White Throne, not to determine whether or not they are saved, but to confirm and to confer upon them punishment for their sin. "My flesh trembleth for fear of thee; and I am afraid of thy judgments."

The psalmist is very explicit. The only way for us to grow spiritual backbone and muscle is to put His Word in our hearts, love Him, and reverence Him. We are to send out of our lives those who would cause us to compromise. We must focus in upon Him. And the church provides us an army of friends, a fellowship that gives strength and courage and leads us on to maturity.

16

Time for God to Work

Psalm 119:121-128

I. **SENSIBLE SUPPLICATION:** vv. 121-123

1. Security: v. 121
2. Surety: v. 122
3. Salvation: v. 123

II. **SUBMISSIVE SERVANT:** vv. 124-125

1. Pity: v. 124
2. Perception: v. 125

III. **SIGNIFICANT STATEMENT:** vv. 126-128

1. Threat: v. 126
2. Treasure: v. 127
3. Truth: v. 128

The situation has not changed for the psalmist. He still has vengeful, persistent enemies surrounding him. He is fed up with it. His impatience is creeping in. We have all been to the place where we have pled, "Enough is enough, Lord. Let's get on with it." The uniqueness of this segment is the impatience of the psalmist and then the fact that in this section is the one verse that does not have a synonym for the Word of God. Every verse but one in Psalm 119 has a synonym for the Scriptures. While the psalmist does not have a synonym for the Word of God, he appeals directly to God Himself in that verse.

He uses the word "servant" three times in these eight verses. The title he gives himself of servant could be a synonym for the personal pronoun "I" or "me." Yet it seems to speak of humility on the part of the psalmist. In the last segment, we beheld the reverence the psalmist had for God and how he respected Him. We still see that reverence in this segment. He knows who God is and he knows who he is, and he responds with a special kind of humility to the Lord.

The psalmist is still having fearful problems with those who hate him and are attacking him, so he turns his appeal to God for security, for surety, and salvation.

"I have done judgment and justice: leave me not to mine oppressors" (v. 121). In this verse we have a veiled hint at the age-old problem of "Why do good people suffer?" It is a seemingly endless problem of right forever on the scaffold and wrong on the throne. It is the struggle where it seems that right fails and wrong triumphs. That is sometimes how it appears to be. In this verse the psalmist contends that he has done the right thing. He is beginning to be impatient of doing what he knows is right, and yet things don't get any better. He is still faced with the oppression of those who hated him.

When we examine the problem of the suffering of the godly, in the short term, there is no answer. Our human minds can never understand in the brief years of this pilgrimage why such takes place, but in the long term, all is going to be well. God is not dead nor is He asleep. His silence is not that of indifference but that of patience. He is still working things together for good. There may still be persecution for God's people, and circumstances may not be what we would like, but God's grace is sufficient for such times, so much so that Paul says, "most gladly therefore will I rather glory in my infirmities, that the power of Christ may rest upon me . . . for when I am weak, then am I strong" (2 Cor. 12:9*b*-10*b*). Our weakness opens the door to God's grace.

In difficulties and problems we open our hearts and become sensitive to the Word of God and God's presence. If we never had a difficulty, we might never turn to God. Most of us coast along until the bottom falls out. Then we turn to God. The problems we face keep our hearts sensitive and tender toward God. That may be part of our answer. And we do know that God is going to give us grace and strength and will not allow evil to triumph.

But the psalmist groans, "Lord, I have done the right thing. Why don't you do something?" He believes that trusting in God makes all the difference. He has fallen on hard times, and others might become weak in their faith or blame God under the same circumstances. But the psalmist has retained his sense of proportion, and he recognizes that diminished faith in God leads only to deeper despair. He also is certain that the triumph of the wicked has to be temporary. Thus, he pleads to God for security. "Don't let my oppressors have their way with me."

Then he asks God to be his surety. This is the verse that does not have a synonym for the Word of God, yet there are ten synonyms in this passage. There is a reason. Throughout this psalm, the psalmist is like a man with a written guarantee that God is going to move mightily in his life, that He will present triumph to his people. The psalmist pulls out that guarantee and reads it, and the more he reads it, the worse things get. Nothing works. He has a guarantee, but it does not seem to be paying dividends. In this verse, he bypasses his guarantee, the written Word, and goes straight to God. That is legitimate for us to do. He has claimed the guarantee and bases his faith on the Word of God; he continues to do that, but now he bypasses his emphasis on the written word and makes an appeal to God Himself. "God, you be the guarantor I need to guide me through this time."

Then he speaks of salvation: "Mine eyes fail for thy salvation" (v. 123). This verse has a quality to it that we need to note. He is saying that he has looked so intently toward God that his eyes are wearing out. Most of us look at our circumstances and do the best we can, and when everything else fails, we run to God and ask Him for help. But the psalmist has been looking for God's salvation from the very start. He has never taken his eyes off God's grace, God's Word, or God's promise from the beginning. His focus on the Word of God and the presence and promise of God is why he could pray, "God, it is time for You to get busy." Only a man who has such a single-minded devotion to the purposes of God for his life would be able to pray with the boldness he does. There is no question his prayers are getting through. He is convinced God is going to act and claims that response from God.

Then he prays as a submissive servant. *Verse 124 speaks of mercy or pity.* "Deal with thy servant according unto thy mercy, and teach me thy statutes" (v. 124). The psalmist links the need for mercy with the need to grasp the laws of God. Mercy and morality go together. God's grace and God's principles of living go hand in hand. The more God does in our lives, the more we want to ascertain what God says and requires. The more God moves in us, the more we want clear instruction from Him.

Verse 125 refers to perception. "I am thy servant; give me understanding, that I may know thy testimonies" (v. 125). The psalmist speaks of himself as a servant. That was a favorite word of the Apostle Paul. He was always calling himself a "bondslave," a "servant." A bondslave was a unique kind of slave in New Testament life. He had been a slave, had been freed, and then had chosen to become a slave again. Paul used that very description for himself. He had decided to be a slave of Jesus Christ. The psalmist has the same sort of commitment. Here is the singer of old, delighted with a sweet captivity to the will and Word of God. He prays for understanding of the will and Word of God.

God is rarely arbitrary with us, even though he has every right to be, somewhat like a parent has that prerogative. How often have we answered our children's question of "Why?" with "Just because I said so"? That should be the end of the conversation. God has that right. He does not have to explain His Word to us, the teachings of the Bible. He can say, "Do it because I say so!"

The psalmist acknowledges the authority of God by calling himself a servant. Now he is asking for understanding. Most of us want to have understanding—then we will decide if we are going to be obedient. But the psalmist says he is obedient first; now he wants understanding. God wants us to yield to His will before we know it. When we have answered "yes" to the will of God even before we know it, we have taken a giant step in our relationship with God. When we reach the place where we say, "Lord, whatever it takes, wherever You want me to be, whatever You want me to do, I will do it," then we have a right to expect answers.

God will provide understanding. His will and Word are not irrational. They are not even illogical. They are suprarational and supralogical. There are times when they transcend rationality and logic. Most of the time, however, God in His grace, imparts understanding when He finds a heart that is yielded to Him. And even more so today. When Jesus left this earth, He sent the Holy Spirit for the purpose of teaching us "all things," guiding us "into all truth." We may expect that, because of the indwelling of the Holy Spirit, we in the New Testament age will understand more. We have a exciting anticipation of having deep insights into His Word and His will.

Now the psalmist sends forth a significant statement. Verse 126 presents a threat. "It is time for thee, Lord, to work: for they have made void thy law" (v. 126). When we tell God it is time for Him to act, we had better be on very certain ground. It takes a very special individual, one who lives close to God, to make an appeal of that nature—only one who walks in fellowship and obedience to God can expect God to work. Why was it time for Him to work? Because wicked men had pushed God out and set aside His Word. His control over human affairs had been undercut and replaced by sinful men. We are rapidly coming to that state in our world today. Men are pushing aside God's laws of decency, morality, and integrity. God must work. He will work in one of several ways. He might work with the Rapture, or He might work with ruin. He could come in a devastating social and economic situation, or He might work with revival. There is such a prevalence of godlessness that it appears it would be very difficult for God to usher in revival—but to the contrary, that is exactly when revival has always come. In a time when evil, wickedness, and lust have no limits, at that time is when God moves dramatically with revival.

The psalmist looked around him and saw the wicked had made void God's word and ridiculed it, so he felt it was high time for God to work. We also need to pray for God to work today. Revival is possible, and we need not be casual about asking for it. It is a serious matter when God sends revival. Almost every great revival in history immediately preceded a crucial national disaster. There is a solemn responsibility when revival comes. When God has sent revival in the past, when He has moved and His power has taken over, when a community has become conscious of God, when lives have been changed and transformed, it nearly always is to prepare those people for intense persecution that is coming.

As we evaluate our lives, none of us can say we don't need God to work in our lives, and we need to listen to this verse. In some area of our lives, perhaps we have made void His law, when we have been disobedient and not allowed God to guide.

The last two verses are so beautiful they almost defy description. "Therefore I love thy commandments above gold; yea, above fine gold" (v. 127). The more men made void the law of God, the more God's people ought to love it. The more people set it aside, the more we ought to embrace it. The more people ignore it, the more we ought to submit to it. The more the world disregards the Word of God, the more we should apply it to every area of our lives.

The Word of God is a treasure. Here is a magnificent claim. He is like a prospector who has struck it rich. The Word of God is more precious than gold to him. His first love was not gold but God. What he desired was not the wealth of the world but the wealth of the Word. When we want the wealth of the Word as much as we want the wealth of the world, God will change our lives with the truth He plants in our hearts.

The psalmist loves God's Word because it affords him a claim on God. When we abide by the Word, it gives us a special claim upon God, His promises, and His integrity. The psalmist is simply exercising his claim by telling God it is time to work. Surely to have a claim on God like that is worth more than all the gold in the world. To be able to approach God with such boldness is an invaluable treasure.

Verse 128 speaks about the truth of the Word of God. "Therefore I esteem all thy precepts concerning all things to be right; and I hate every false way." Whatever God's Word says is right concerning everything. We ought to stand on that. The previous verse puts a *monetary value* on the Bible. This verse puts a *moral value* on the Bible. It is always right. Regardless of whether we understand it or whether we think it is right, it is always right.

I received a letter from an elderly man in Richmond, Virginia. He had found a "contradiction" in the Bible, and he quoted these two statements about the death of one of God's servants in the Old Testament. In one place it said he fell on his sword and killed himself, and in another, that the enemy killed him. The second report claiming he was killed by the enemy was a false claim by the enemy. The Bible does record false statements made by individuals. When the Bible makes statements, they are true. The false statement of the individual was an accurate account of what he said—it was just that the man lied! It is not a contradiction. The Bible recorded it accurately, truthfully. The so-called "discrepancies" in the Bible are not new. The so-called "errors" in the Bible have been discussed for nearly 2,000 years. We are not the first generation to ask questions, to single out possible paradoxes and contradictions. That has been done from the first century onward, and gifted scholars down through the ages have adequately answered all of them. We cannot improve on what the psalmist writes here. "Therefore I esteem all thy precepts concerning all things to be right." That is the conclusion any honest scholar will make. If he comes to the Word of God with faith, trusting God and allowing Him to reveal truth to him, that will be his conclusion. Whatever God says is right.

Let the world trot out its religions and its cults. If what they say is a contradiction to the truth of the Bible, then let God be true and everyone else be a liar. Whenever God speaks to us about creation, regardless of how many pictures magazines print as though they had a photographer on the scene when the world "evolved," if God says it was created, that's how it happened. Whatever God's Word says to us about crime and human nature, that settles it. Whatever God's Word tells us about human conduct is correct. Whatever He says about conversion and how to know Him is right. That's how it is. You can count on it, base your life on it, and put your faith in it.

Let's be truthful. Our problem with the Bible is not with what we don't understand; *it is with what we do understand and are not willing to obey.* We all know to do more than we do. Whatever God says, on whatever issue He speaks, is right. Some say that conviction makes us bigots. I say it makes us believers. God's Word is worth investing our lives in, obeying whatever He tells us to do. "Whatsoever he saith unto you, do it" (John 2:5). We put our faith and trust in Christ because the Bible tells us that is how to come to God. We are baptized because the Bible tells us it is a witness to what has happened in our hearts. It becomes a testimony of our faith in Jesus Christ. It is an outward picture of an inward change.

We are faithful stewards of our possessions because God's Word tells us "it is required in stewards that a man be found faithful" (1 Cor. 4:2). We are devoted witnesses of the gospel of Jesus Christ because the Word of God tells us we are responsible to those who do not know Jesus Christ. We help support missions around the world. My denomination has more than 7,300 full-time career missionaries at home and abroad because the Word of God instructed us to do it. We cannot be true to our calling from God unless we do what God tells us to do. We will never go wrong basing our lives on what God has said, being obedient to what He has revealed.

17

The Wonderful Word of God

Psalm 119:129-136

I. **DEVOTION:** vv. 129-130

   1. Obedience: v. 129
   2. Opportunity: v. 130

II. **DESIRE:** vv. 131-133

   1. Guided: vv. 131-132
   2. Guarded: v. 133

III. **DELIVERANCE:** vv. 134-135

   1. Rescue: v. 134
   2. Response: v. 135

IV. **DISTRESS:** v. 136

   1. Tears: v. 136*a*
   2. Tumult: v. 136*b*

The major thrust of this particular section is: The Word of God conveys manifold blessings, and therefore we ought to keep faithfully its commandments. This is so because of what it does, how it meets our needs, and because of the blessings we receive through the Word. Thus, we ought to be faithful and meticulous in keeping the commandments of our Lord.

The first part deals with obedience. "Thy testimonies are won-

derful: therefore doth my soul keep them. The entrance of thy
words giveth light; it giveth understanding unto the simple"
(vv. 129-130). This is a sublime statement. "Thy word is wonderful!" The Word is wonderful in its scope or its sufficiency because
it meets our every need now and later. It is wonderful in its simplicity because even the youngest child can understand it and receive it. It is wonderful in its wisdom. It is the wisest book of all.
It is wonderful in its accuracy, truth, and comfort; wonderful in its
anticipation, its praise, its eternal quality; wonderful in the message of salvation. It is effective, instructional, complete. It is wonderful in giving us power, answers, and cleansing. Wonderful!!!
The Word of God is the substance of everything God has revealed
to us. All we know about God of a personal nature we know
through the Word of God. We can know generally certain concepts
about God, His mighty power as we observe creation, but everything specific we know about God, salvation, eternity, forgiveness, peace, joy, satisfaction, and the like is through the Word of
God.

It is no wonder the psalmist exulted, "Thy testimonies are *wonderful*." It is so exciting to consider its relevance and guiding
power in our lives. We will never go wrong following its precepts.

". . . Therefore, doth my soul keep them." Because we believe
it is wonderful, we abide by its teachings. Remember Jesus'
words, "And why call ye me, Lord, Lord, and do not the things
which I say?" (Luke 6:46). Why do we claim the Bible is wonderful and yet not obey it? The proof of our attitude toward the Word
of God is that we use it as our rule for life. We must place alongside the Word of God every decision, every relationship, every
situation. It should dictate our actions and attitudes. We should
keep its testimonies because it is wonderful.

It offers wonderful opportunity for us. "The entrance of thy
words giveth light" (v. 129). As we read and study the Word of
God, light comes to our soul. We can shut out the light. We can
choose to live in darkness, or we can open the windows of our soul
and let the light in. When we allow the light of God to enter, a

wonderful opportunity is ours. What does light do? *Light, first of all, reveals dirt.* As sun streaming through a window will reflect thousands of dust particles in what we thought was clean air, the Word will reveal that which is displeasing to God in our lives. It will expose the dirt in our lives.

Not only that, it reveals the true condition of a room. Just as we can keep the light off in a room, we can refuse to let it shine upon our attitudes, our actions, and our relationships. We can keep it hidden. But if we let the light in, it will reveal what really is there. It will reveal the disorder or order of a room, and it will do the same with our hearts.

Light also reveals direction. A man stumbling around in the dark may not know where he is, but if we turn the light on, and he finds perspective. He is able to identify where he is and what to do. The Word of God is like that. Many of us are groping through life, trying to make sense out of nonsense, when all we have to do is turn on the light of God's Word. That is our opportunity. The Word of God is wonderful and there is a wonderful devotion we can have because of its wonder. And because it is wonderful we should take advantage of the opportunity to let it be light in our hearts.

". . . It giveth understanding unto the simple" (v. 130*b*). It does not say it gives understanding to the sophisticated or the highly educated. It says "the simple." There are many who are "too clever" to believe the Bible, too enamored with their own intelligence, their own understanding. They have what Paul warned about: "Beware lest any man spoil you through philosophy and vain deceit, after the tradition of men, after the rudiments of the world, and not after Christ" (Col. 2:8). There are many folks like that. J. B. Phillips, in his translation of this passage, calls it "intellectualism or high-sounding nonsense." What sounds intelligent to the human mind is actually man's limited perspective. Any time anyone talks to us in arbitrary terms about eternal matters, they are of necessity speaking from a narrow framework. Paul warns against letting anyone mess us up with intellectualism and high-sounding nonsense. God gives understanding to the "simple" and to the teachable, and all of us are simple before Him. The Bible has little or nothing to say to people who want to argue or contradict. The Bible was not handed to us as a starting point for debate but as the starting point for obedience. Do it! Obey it! It gives understanding. Is it any wonder an honest look at the Word of God calls for devotion?

Then we see a desire. "I opened my mouth, and panted: for I longed for thy commandments. Look thou upon me, and be merciful unto me, as thou usest to do unto those that love thy name. Order my steps in thy word: and let not any iniquity have dominion over me" (vv. 131-133). His desire was that he be guided by the Word of God. He uses the picture of a wild animal about to die of thirst: panting. One day I was playing golf in Albuquerque, New Mexico. It was 100 degrees in the shade. And it was a *hot* hot! I felt we were about to die of the heat. As we approached the sixteenth hole and the end of the day, we noticed a rabbit under a little, scroungy-looking bush. I always remember rabbits sitting up with their ears perked, darting away when they noticed someone watching them. This little fellow was flat on his stomach with his legs outstretched, and he was panting from the heat and thirst. We walked right up on a wild rabbit, and all he could do was lie there, panting for water. The psalmist feels like that about the Word of God. It is as though every drop of truth from the Word of God is a priceless one that quenches thirst. The writer pants for it and longs for it.

That puts to shame our indifference toward the Word of God. His longing was not excessive; ours is defective. We do not hunger enough for the Word of God. The truth is that most of us ignore the Word of God. Most of us have two or three—maybe even a dozen—Bibles, but we don't open them. Many martyrs have paid a precious price to allow us to hold in our hands the Word of God. Scholars gave their lives to translate it. Yet we yawn indifferently, and our thoughts wander. We do not pant for the Word of God. We would appreciate it only if it were taken away from us. It is a shame that we would have to lose it before we could understand its value and appreciate it.

John Wycliffe died in the fourteenth century, and forty or fifty years after he died, "religious" people dug up his bones and burned them. That is how much they hated him. What had he done? He had translated the Bible! They tossed some of his ashes in the air, buried some of them, and scattered the rest onto a river. They thought they had done away with Wycliffe. What they did not know is that nothing could destroy him and his influence, and we are the richer today because Wycliffe loved the Bible and sought to translate it for us.

The father of our modern Bible translations, credited with giving us the English translation, was William Tyndale. Toward the end of his life he was thrown into jail for translating the Bible. History records that he led his jailkeeper, his jailkeeper's wife and daughter, and many others in that household to Christ. The soldiers who kept him were quoted as saying, "If this man is not a Christian, we do not know where to find one." Because of his love for the Bible and his desire to translate it into English, he was thrown into prison. One old chronicle has recorded:

> At last after much reasoning when no reason would serve although he deserved no death, he was condemned by virtue of the Emperor's decree made in the Assembly at Augburg. He was brought forth to the place of execution, he was tied to the stake, strangled by the hangman and afterwards, consumed by fire at the town of Vilvord, A.D. 1536, crying at the stake with a fervent zeal and a loud voice, "Lord, open the King of England's eyes." As touching his translation of the New Testament, because his enemies did so much to carp at it, pretending it to be full of heresies, he wrote to John Frith as follows: "I call God to record against the day when we shall appear before our Lord Jesus that I never altered one syllable of God's Word against my conscience, nor would do this day if all that is in this earth, whether it be honor, pleasure or riches might be given me."

This English Bible that means so little to us came at a steep price. It cost in blood, tears, and death. The psalmist longed for it, panted for it. How important for us to have that kind of desire, to be guided by the Word of God!

"Look thou upon me, and be merciful unto me, as thou usest to do unto those that love thy name"(v. 132). There are three statements about God in this verse. *First, he says God is able to see. Second, he says that God is able to save:* "Be merciful to me." *And third, he says that God is immutable, always the same:* ". . . as thou usest to do unto those that love thy name." In other words, God is consistent, always the same in His relationship to us. He is no respecter of persons. *What a desire ought to be in our hearts for the Word of God.*

"Deliver me from the oppression of man: so will I keep thy precepts. Make thy face to shine upon thy servant; and teach me thy statutes" (vv. 134-35). *He wants God to rescue him.* Apparently, when he speaks of being delivered from oppression, he is in a place where it is very difficult to be true to God's Word. Everyone of us has been in a situation where our integrity, our morality, and our ethics have been tested, in a place where it would have been easier not to do what God wanted. Young people face it every day at school. Businessmen grapple with it every day at work. Each of us in our homes, wherever we might be, face it all the time. The psalmist wanted to be rescued. He wanted deliverance from the situation where it was hard for him to keep God's precepts.

Then he asks for this response from God: "Make thy face to shine upon thy servant; and teach me thy statutes" (v. 135). The sun is always shining. Even when we cannot see it, it is shining up there. So, the face of our Lord is always shining upon us. There are times when it seems obscured, when circumstances threaten our consciousness of God's presence. The psalmist feels that a dark cloud has somehow come between God and him, obscuring God's shining face. All of us have been where we felt God was separated from us, that He was not hearing us. We have waited anxiously for God to respond, but He hasn't done so. We cannot understand why. It seems as though He has turned His face away from us, and we have cried as the psalmist did, "Make thy face to shine upon thy servant."

But notice he added: ". . . and teach me thy statutes." We all want God to smile upon our lives in an evident way, but if we want that smile, we must allow God to teach us His ways, His statutes. God will smile on us only when we live consistently with His teachings in His Word. To experience God in our lives, we must live in the will of God.

The last verse is one of the most remarkable in the entire section. *It speaks of his distress.* All of a sudden, his eyes are filled with tears as he looks about him and sees tumult. "Rivers of waters run down mine eyes, because they keep not thy law" (v. 136). He has talked about how wonderful the Word of God is and how it has given us a marvelous revelation. *All of a sudden he bursts into tears.*

Why is he crying? He is weeping for three things. *First of all, he is weeping for his enemies.* He does more than pray for them— he weeps over them. Do we weep over those who hate us, pray with tears for those who despise us? That is tough. Face it. Are there some people we would love for the Lord to "zap"? But here the psalmist wept for them.

Then he weeps for God. He cries over the rebellion that is being transmitted and what it does to the heart of a loving God. God's heart breaks when we sin by not keeping His Word. When a society becomes lawless, He doesn't become angry over it—He weeps over it. The psalmist weeps over his own society and what it is doing to God.

Then he weeps for his world. He realizes what sin does to a society, and he weeps over the tumult that always follows when God is disobeyed. Sin has plowed this planet with sorrow and grief; rebellion against God has planted every graveyard on this earth. Sin has made necessary every hospital, every prison, every psychiatric unit in this world; it has conceived and built every slum. When we make void the law of God, we flood the earth with woes. Were it not for sin, we could disband the armies, dissolve the police forces, open the prisons, dismiss the legislatures, and unlock our doors. He weeps over what sin does in a world. Jesus wept on the Mount of Olives over the ravages of sin in Jerusalem, the city He loved. So did the psalmist. Who weeps over our cities? Who weeps over our state, our nation? Who weeps because of the rebellion in our world against God?

When was the last time we wept over a concern that wasn't selfish. When was the last time we wept over another person?

The psalmist starts out by rejoicing in God's testimonies as wonderful. As he thinks further about the wonderful Word of God, he recognizes there is the flip side: If we disregard this Word, we sow seeds of terrible distress, grief, and suffering. What began as praise over the wondrous Word ends up with "rivers of tears" flowing down his face concerning his enemies, concerning God's broken heart, and concerning a dying world.

We should never rest until we are gripped with that kind of concern. As the Prophet Jeremiah lamented, "Oh that my head were waters, and mine eyes a fountain of tears that I might weep day and night for the slain of the daughter of my people!" (Jer. 9:1).

18

God's Integrity Is Sure

Psalm 119:137-144

I. **PROPRIETY:** vv. 137-138

   1. Immutability: v. 137
   2. Instruction: v. 138

II. **PERSPECTIVE:** vv. 139-141

   1. Industry: v. 139
   2. Intensity: vv. 140-141

III. **PROTECTION:** vv. 142-143

   1. Scripture: v. 142
   2. Suffering: v. 143

IV. **PROVISION:** v. 144

The focal point of this segment is the integrity of God, what He has said. His Word is right; what He tells us is true. It is consistent and faithful and will always lead us in the right direction. Thus, the general theme of this segment is God's integrity or His divine righteousness.

The first two verses describe the propriety of the Word of God, the rightness of it. It is impossible for God to do anything wrong— whatever God does is right. Verse 137 speaks of the immutability of God's Word, the fact that it will always be the same. "Righteous art thou, O Lord, and upright are thy judgments." In the character of God and His commands—and in everything God does and says—He is always right. Whatever He speaks to us about, He is always correct. If He speaks to instruct us, it is right. What we understand may seem to contradict it, but when all the facts are in, God's Word will be proven right.

A good example is, for instance, that the Bible clearly teaches that the world is a sphere and hangs on nothing in space. That contradicted human science for many centuries. For many centuries, people thought the world was flat, that there came a place where you fell off. We have seen the Word of God vindicated. What it said was right. The earth is indeed a sphere and hangs on nothing in space. Man's understanding was proven wrong, and God's Word, right. When God's Word contradicts what man says, believe God.

When He speaks to prohibit us, what He urges us not to do is always the correct action for us. God's Word does have prohibitions for us. It speaks at great length on human conduct. The Bible teaches us what kind of conduct should not be engaged in by people who want to receive the most satisfying and fulfilling experiences of life. We are counseled to be pure sexually, and that any immorality is a sin against the body. We are warned that perversion is against God's way, whether it be homosexuality or any other sexual deviation so prevalent today. Man's society insists these sins are all right. God's Word makes it plain they are wrong. Understand that when God prohibits us, He is right. He does it in order to protect us and also for us to get the most out of life. We do not have to understand it to be aware that it is in our best interest not to do what God forbids.

If God speaks to inspire us or to challenge us, it is always right. The highest, happiest, holiest destiny possible is in conformity to the Word of God. Any other concept or encouragement to do otherwise is wrong. God's way is always right.

"Thy testimonies that thou hast commanded are righteous and very faithful" (v. 138). This verse tells us that, when God gives us specific instructions, a path to follow, He will never ask us to do something wrong or that will lead us astray. We must understand that God's will is not open for vote. He is never swayed by public opinion. He does not run the universe by democratic processes. His testimonies are righteous and very faithful, and whenever He commands us to do something, it is not for public approval.

God gives us a wealth of instruction. He talks to us about morality, politics, social issues, sex, sanitation, stealing; diet and dress, family and finances, warfare and welfare. And whatever He tells us is right. His instructions are always righteous. The psalmist says "very" faithful. How can you be more than faithful? But the psalmist goes further by saying "very faithful." God's instructions are unchangeable. *There is an immutability about them, a propriety about what God says.*

Verses 139 to 141 offer us a perspective. "My zeal hath consumed me, because mine enemies have forgotten thy words. Thy word is very pure: therefore thy servant loveth it. I am small and despised: yet do not I forget thy precepts." *First, we see the industry of the psalmist.* He looks and sees how men are disregarding God, and it upsets him. The friction between what God says to do and what godless men are doing causes his zeal to consume him. That is a picture of powerful intensity. He is angry, not because of what his enemies are doing to him, but because of what they are doing against God. He is jealous for God. In his agitation and distress he wails, "I am consumed in my zeal."

It should always be like that. The tragedy is when we become so accustomed to men's evil ways that they no longer bother us or upset us. It is tragic when we become calloused to men's godlessness, and it does not distress our spirit or cause us to be jealous or zealous for God. He sees his own devotion and sets it in contrast to his enemies' forgetfulness of God.

He might pray for his enemies, as he does from time to time. He might even pity them, but his soul is stirred at what they are doing. His contempt for them is because of their sneering attitude toward God. Too often, the church is not only not zealous for God, it is not even upset at how the world treats God.

The psalmist is running to God's defense, and he is intense in his enthusiasm, his zeal for God. We need to be so single-minded where we stand for God, and we recognize what stands against God. We must not lose our sensitivity about evil and unrighteousness. Some of us may remember the first time we heard someone curse and how we felt. The first time I heard someone take God's name in vain, it shocked and revolted me. Now that has become so common that many don't notice it anymore. One of the classic examples of our day would be the motion picture industry. There was a time when a committed Christian would not even go to a movie, especially if it contradicted the Christian way of life. Now we have ratings for bad language, violence, and sex. Those kinds of movies frequently use four-letter words and God's name in vain. And I have heard Christians talking about what wonderful movies they are. How can we become calloused to men's attitudes toward God and cease to be sensitive to what is right and proper. It is an old pattern of becoming insensitive to that which we are accustomed to hearing and seeing. The psalmist moans, "I can't get used to it. I see men forgetting God, turning against Him. I watch it, and my zeal eats me alive."

He did not attack these people. His distress drove him to greater zeal for God, a greater obedience. We ought to do more every day of what God calls us to do, to be more of what God would have us to be, and to act as God expects us to act. The psalmist was doing precisely this. Because of what his enemies had done toward God, he became more committed and obedient—consumed with zeal.

Being a Christian ought to be a compulsion. It ought to drive us. We ought to be people with convictions, not opinions. Our commitment should cause us to stand firm and stand tall in our relationship to Jesus Christ. We are prone to compromise the demands of faith. We forget that Jesus Himself said, "If you don't love Me more than anyone else in the world, you cannot be My disciple. If you do not count the cost, take up your cross, and follow me, you cannot be My disciple" (see Luke 14:26*ff.*). He did not say "shouldn't be" or "ought not be," but He stressed, "You *cannot* be my disciple." Here is a challenge to an intense, irrevocable commitment to Him.

The psalmist expresses this kind of devotion. He could not avoid his reverence and love for God. We need a good dose of righteous indignation in our day. We often tolerate everything and anything under the name of being "broadminded" and "accepting different views." In the name of plurality and diversity, we accept everything until we stand for nothing. The psalmist held fast to his convictions.

This intensity continues as he looks at the Word of God. "Thy word is very pure: therefore thy servant loveth it" (v. 140). The word "pure" means "thoroughly refined." Thus, it is pure because it is thoroughly refined like precious metal smelted in the furnace. God's Word is not pure because it is refined; it is refined and pure because it is God's Word. God is the Author. It can be nothing less than pure because of who the author is. The psalmist loves God's Word because it is so pure. It provides a picture of drinking pure water. God's Word is so pure we can drink from it and not worry about contamination. It is purity embodied because God has written it. Man's ideas pollute us. We will have a bad reaction to some of the water available without discernment, but we can imbibe the Word of God, and it will never defile us.

Then, his enemies come back into focus and he speaks of his troubles. "I am small and despised: yet do not I forget thy precepts" (v. 141). J. B. Phillips notes that there are three brief statements the psalmist makes about himself. First, "I am small." That causes him to throw himself on the bigness of God. Then he says, "I am scorned." Phillips further observes that small people are often scorned. Then he says, "I am smart." "In spite of the fact that I am small and scorned, I don't forget God's precepts. I am a smart man." The fact that he is scorned and despised, and that his troubles abound, does not cause him to abandon the Word of God. It pushes him closer. This is a rich perspective about the Word of God.

In verses 142-143 we find the protection the Word of God offers. "Thy righteousness is an everlasting righteousness, and thy law is the truth. Trouble and anguish have taken hold on me: yet thy commandments are my delights." Righteousness is the quality of God that causes Him always to do and say what is right. He does not only act righteously, He *is* righteousness. Because of His character, He says and does that which is right. Whatever God does is correct. If God decides to create a universe with millions of galaxies and heavenly bodies, then that is right. We may not understand why, but we can rest assured that it was the right for Him to do it. His righteousness is that quality which always causes Him to do what is right. Since He decided to create man, without our understanding, it was right. If He created angels to serve Him separate from man, angels who are more mechanical than man with his free will, then it was right. Whatever God does is right. His *right*-eousness is everlasting. We do not know much; we are not too smart. So, it is not important that we understand. God's righteousness is everlasting.

That indicates that the righteousness of God underlies all that is in the Bible. If we want to ascertain what is right about anything, all we have to do is find out what the Bible says about it. When we discover that, it is right. That takes all the pressure off of us. There is a glowing testimony to Scripture here. God's *right*-eousness, the element that always causes Him to say and do what is right, is everlasting in its nature.

Then he speaks again of suffering. That is a recurring theme. Trouble and anguish threaten all of us, and none of us likes to see them coming. When we hear them knock at our door, we don't want to answer. They are often Satan's tools to imprison, to ensnare, and to enslave us. How do we rid ourselves of them? The best way is to emulate the psalmist: ". . . Yet thy commandments are my delights." If we delight in the Word of God, we will rid ourselves of the domination trouble and anguish have over us. The depression that comes when we are dominated by our circumstances is lifted when we delight in the Word of God. "Even though trouble and anguish are upon me, I have found the commandments of God to be my delight." That is how we are to silence the pressure of trouble and anguish and prove that trouble cannot silence the song that God places in the human heart.

The last verse speaks of the provision God makes. "The righteousness of thy testimonies is everlasting: give me understanding, and I shall live" (v. 144). The Bible is constructed of the same stuff eternity is made of. It transcends time. It will outlast the universe. It was hammered out of the eternal ages. It is the very breath of God. Jesus said, "Heaven and earth shall pass away: but my words will not pass away" (Mark 13:31). The psalmist wrote earlier in this psalm, "Forever, O Lord, thy word is established in heaven" (v. 89). That is the Holy Spirit's witness to the provision of God's Word. The righteousness of God and the Bible, the Word of God, will outlast time.

No wonder the psalmist breaks into a song: "Give me understanding, and I shall live." The word "understanding" points back to the testimonies of God. He is not talking about general understanding of nature or the laws of this world. Rather, he is asking for comprehension of what God has said. When we understand the testimonies of God—and that is the work of the Holy Spirit in our lives—then we will live.

Everlasting life is inherent in the Word of God. It can be transmitted to the human soul. In Genesis, the Scripture records how God spoke and the world came into being. In Hebrews 11 it says, "Through faith we understand that the worlds were framed by the word of God"(v. 3*a*). God spoke, and it happened. "Let there be light, and there was light." God breathed into Adam, and Adam became "a living soul." Physical life came when God breathed into him. Peter says in the New Testament that we are "born again, not of corruptible seed, but of incorruptible, by the word of God . . ." (1 Pet. 2:23). Paul says in 2 Timothy that the Word of God is "God-breathed." When God gave us His Word, He breathed through those men and breathed out His Holy Word (see 2 Tim. 3:16-17). When that Word is placed in the heart of a human being, he who is a living soul because of the breath of God in our ancestor Adam, becomes a living spiritual being. Salvation takes place, and we are born again by the Word of God.

By God's Word, man became a living being with personality, strength, intelligence, and communication skills. God breathed that into Adam and his descendants. Now, God takes His Word and literally breathes that Word into the spirit of individuals. The Word of God "births" us and causes us to come alive spiritually. "And you hath he quickened, who were dead in trespasses and sins" (Eph. 2:1). By the Word of God we were made alive, demonstrated through Jesus Christ on the cross, revealed in the record He has provided for us. *The Word of God becomes God's provision for our lives*. We can trust it. If we abide by it, we will always experience and know happiness, fulfillment, and satisfaction. We will never make a mistake choosing what God's Word requests of us. It is a marvelous truth. God's Word is right and will always usher blessings into our lives.

If we lay our lives alongside the Word of God, if we search the Scriptures and let them flow into our hearts, we will be strong in our Christian faith. Today we want instant maturity. Our society encourages such. Someone who has any popularity at all gets saved, and the next night we have him giving his testimony. What does he know? Not much! He doesn't know the things of God. He does know he was saved. We need to grow and mature in our faith, and the way to do that is to spend time in the Word of God. Read it, study it, memorize it, quote it. When Satan tempted Jesus, He quoted Scripture as His defense. Pour the Word of God into your heart and your mind. God will save you through His Word if that is your need. It will sustain you after you have been saved, and it will direct your life. What a marvelous Word we have!

19

When the Heart Cries

Psalm 119:145-153

I. **AFFECTION:** vv. 145-146

    1. Desperation: v. 145
    2. Depression: v. 146

II. **ACTION:** vv. 147-148

    1. Morning: v. 147
    2. Midnight: v. 148

III. **APPEAL:** v. 149

    1. Love: v. 149*a*
    2. Life: v. 149*b*

IV. **ATTITUDE:** vv. 150-152

    1. Treachery: v. 150
    2. Truth: vv. 151-152

In this passage the psalmist is still in adverse circumstances, still raising his voice in cries of desperate appeal, praying to God for help. The cries are not new. He has been crying out to God continually and wholeheartedly, combining his prayer with resolves and with obedience. Nearly always when the psalmist prays, he petitions God to move amid his circumstances and at the same time pledges to God that he will be true to what God tells him to do. This passage is similar to several we have seen before.

"I cried with my whole heart; hear me, O Lord: I will keep thy statutes. I cried unto thee; save me, and I shall keep thy testimonies" (vv. 145-146). *These two verses deal with his affection.* They speak of tremendous emotion. There is a fervor about his cry to God, a zeal about his prayer. There are all kinds of cries. A child cries for different reasons. A mother ignores some cries. Sometimes a child cries just because it is mad or wants attention. Sometimes it is a peevish cry or a whine, a spoiled variety of crying. Then there is the "other" kind of crying. It is the sort of cry that gets everyone's attention. It is the cry of pain and desperation. We learn to recognize the difference between different cries. One thing is sure: When we hear the cry of desperate pain, we always respond. We give our immediate attention.

And that is the sort of cry the psalmist is raising. He is frightened. He is in pain and agony and in need of help. There is a poignancy about this cry, and a loving Heavenly Father always responds to that kind of cry. God is certainly going to be more responsive than an earthly parent. When there is a desperate cry on the part of God's children, God always responds.

Someone has said, "The beginning place of prayer is desperation." When we become absolutely desperate for a message from God, for an answer from God, when we are at the end of our rope, then we really begin to pray. The Book of James says that Elijah was "a man of like passions as we are." That means he had the same kind of emotions, temperament, and temptations we have. Alexander Whyte, speaking of Elijah, wrote that not only was Elijah a man of like passions as we are, but he was also a man who took those passions and put them into his prayers. When he prayed, he prayed with a deep, fervent zeal, with a holy sense of desperation that allowed him to lay hold of God. He knew how to pray with his whole heart.

Notice that he put a promise with his prayer. These are two solid ingredients in genuine praying. These are the emotional ingredient and the volitional ingredient. The emotional says, "I am desperate." The volitional says, "I am determined." The emotional says,

"Rescue me." The volitional says, "I choose to follow You." Those are two good ingredients in prayer. It is the helpless desperation of an emotional being reaching out to God and the steadfast determination to honor God in one's life. The psalmist makes this approach in his prayer.

This leads him to action: "I prevented the dawning of the morning, and cried: I hoped in thy word" (v. 147). The word "prevented" means "anticipated" or "forestalled." It also means "prolonged." We all know how that happens. If we don't sleep, it seems as though morning never comes. He slowed the process of the dawning of the morning by not being able to sleep. Verses 147 and 148 indicate he was very persistent. He prayed and kept on praying. He knocked, and he kept on knocking until he pounded heaven with his request. He was persistent and forestalled the morning coming. His fervent prayers to God seemed to put off the dawn.

We have all been in that place, worrying, fearful, desperate, insomniac, sleep driven from our eyes. When one arises in the morning after being awake all night, every bone and every joint in one's body aches. When we lie on the bed tossing and turning, the night seems so long. The psalmist describes that when he says, "I prevented the morning from coming."

"Mine eyes prevent the night watches, that I might meditate in thy word" (v. 148). Now at midnight, before he goes to bed, he uses that time praying to God, meditating on the Word of God. He employs the word "prevent" again. Before he would turn to sleep at night, he used those moments to meditate upon the truth God had given him. He "redeemed" the time. It is a picture of not wasting a moment. We waste so much time. If we live to be seventy-five years old, we will spend twenty-three years of it sleeping. But here is a man willing to give up some sleep in order to think about God, to commune with Him. He uses every moment wisely.

God offers each of us one fleeting moment of time. Once it is gone, it never returns again. We all have the same amount of time.

No one has more time than we have. We all have twenty-four hours a day, sixty minutes in each hour, sixty seconds in each minute. But how do we use it? The psalmist says he uses that time when he lies upon his bed, and normally would be waiting for sleep to come, to quote Scripture, to memorize Scripture, to meditate on Scripture. When he awakens in the middle of the night, rather than waiting to go back to sleep, he cries out to God, taking advantage of every moment. Do you see the intensity, the seriousness of it? We all have this time given to us. We can seize it and use it in a way that will profit eternity, or we can give it back to God, unredeemed and wasted, and it will become a testimony against us when we stand at the judgment seat of Christ. Life's golden moments never return.

It is sad that we allow Satan to rob us of so much of life. When we are young, he tells us to wait until we are a little older. He tells us not to get too serious now, that we need to enjoy ourselves, "do our thing." Then we marry, and Satan tells us we need to spend our time getting to know each other. Then we have children, and Satan again tells us we don't have time to become serious with God. We believe that lie, and our children grow up. When they reach about eleven or twelve, we discover we are chauffeurs, not parents. We spend our time going to and fro with our family. Now we don't have time for God for sure, so we put it off until they are grown.

Satan causes us to put off getting serious with God to another time, letting this time slip by. Every moment we lose we never regain. We had better do what we can while we can. Stop and smell the roses. Get right with God. Do what He tells you to do. Concentrate on the things that count, because we will wake up one of these days and fifty years will have passed—And we will have nothing to our credit. Every moment we lose, we never reclaim. The psalmist wanted God so much that before he went to sleep at night he meditated on the Word of God. When he awoke in the middle of the night, he cried to God and prayed unto Him. We are so insensitive, so careless about spiritual things, but the psalmist is deadly serious. He is desperate as he cries unto the Father.

In verse 149 he makes his appeal: "Hear my voice according unto thy lovingkindness: O Lord, quicken me according to thy judgment" (v. 149). The psalmist makes two salient points in this verse. *First, he wants the Lord to hear him on the basis of His love.* Notice he says, "Hear *my* voice." Putting that into today's context, we can see how significant that is. There are five billion people in the world today. Many of them are crying out to God, and we want him to hear our voice? Only God can hear the multitude of voices at the same time and not be confused by them. Only God can hear them and make understanding out of them.

Not only does he want Him to respond in love, but in life. "Quicken me" means to "make alive." He bases his petitions on the steadfast love of God and the correct and proper judgment of God. His appeal is for God to hear his voice in love and in life.

Once again he paints the picture of his enemies. "They draw nigh [near] that follow after mischief: they are far from thy law." Near and far are apt to describe these enemies of the psalmist. They are far away from God, but they are near the psalmist. They are after him. They are intent on mischief and motivated by malice. When we have folks like that after us, there is only one defense—God! Their distance from God contributed largely to their being what they were. There is an evident contrast intended here. These men were far from God, but God is near to his believer. The truth of God's presence is all that really counts.

"Thou art near, O Lord; and all thy commandments are truth. Concerning thy testimonies, I have known of old that thou hast founded them forever" (vv. 151-152). When we know that God is near and that God's Word is truth, we can look without fear into the faces of our enemies, whoever they may be or whatever they may say. In the previous verse the psalmist told us his enemies were near. Now he testifies that God is near, and that is enough. That was all he needed. It would be easier for everything else to fail than for God's Word to fail. His Word is true and unfailing.

And he concludes by saying that God's Word is forever. Back before God's Holy Spirit ever inspired Moses to write the first line of the Book of Genesis, before God created Adam and Eve, before there was a world as we know it, back in the silence of eternity past, God's Word was there. God did not think up this or that and then put it in the Bible. What is in the Bible is and always has been the Word of God. It has always been there, forever. Forever past. However far back we can go, His Word was there even before that—and forever future. Beyond the rapture of the church, beyond the millennium, beyond Armageddon, beyond the judgment, beyond eternity future, God's Word is established.

How. long will God's Word endure? It will view the burial of all its enemies. It will still be here. It is a Word we can trust forever.

20

The Afflictions of the Righteous

Psalm 119:153-160

I. **PERSISTENT AFFLICTION:** vv. 153-154

    1. Appraisal: v. 153
    2. Advocate: v. 154

II. **PRECISE ASSESSMENT:** vv. 155-156

    1. Pursuit: v. 155
    2. Provision: v. 156

III. **PERNICIOUS ATTACKERS:** vv. 157-158

    1. Gravity: v. 157
    2. Grief: v. 158

IV. **PROPER ATTITUDE:** vv. 159-160

    1. Devotion: v. 159
    2. Declaration: v. 160

Once again, the psalmist is preoccupied with his persecutors and the opposition he is facing. For a moment we find him back in the valley, but he doesn't stay there for long. He moves on and beyond the valley. One phrase in this section appears three times. It is "quicken me." It would be profitable for us to think about the matter of being quickened, being revived, being made to live again, or to come alive according to the Word of God (v. 154), according to the judgments of God (v. 156), and according to the lovingkindness or grace of God (v. 159). Those are three aspects of the Christian life worthy of close study.

This passage is very applicable to our lives. The psalmist is surrounded by people he once counted as friends, people he loves deeply. They have betrayed him, and he feels isolated and lonely. But rather than being driven from God's Word, from obedience to God, he is driven to the Word of God. In his conclusion he bases his life on that solid foundation.

"Consider mine affliction, and deliver me: for I do not forget thy law. Plead my cause, and deliver me: quicken me according to thy word" (vv. 153-154). William Cowper calls these afflictions "the frowning providence." It is as hard to ignore a "frowning providence" as a toothache. We certainly cannot forget it. We wonder why the psalmist keeps coming back to his problems. They have not gone away. No amount of pretending can make them go away. When we have the kind of oppositions and afflictions he has, we cannot merely push them away. That is why he keeps coming back to them.

There is one blessing that comes from this nagging providence, this aching he cannot turn loose of, and that is a new sense of dependence on God. The problems we face are our friends if they keep us close to God. Every time the psalmist confronts opposition, affliction, and disappointment, such pushes him closer to God.

He makes an appraisal in verse 153, pointing out an important truth: Not all suffering and affliction are punitive. Every time we have some form of suffering or affliction, it does not mean we are being punished by God. A growing segment of the Christian community thinks otherwise. They believe if you are sick, it must be because there is some sin in your life. To them, sickness is considered incompatible with spirituality. If we only had sufficient faith, there would be an instant and miraculous healing. That sounds good, but everyone who has believed that (who is not still living) has died, of course. It is a real tragedy when a funeral destroys your theology. People still die. Most die from some definite cause. Very few of them just wear out. There is an affliction that causes it. God works through suffering. I don't like suffering, but I'm not willing to blame my suffering on a lack of faith that puts the responsibility on some goodness I can generate to please God. That is a distortion of Scripture.

The Word of God does not equate health and wealth with spirituality. In fact, the Sermon on the Mount begins with a series of Beatitudes that would make the positive thinkers and the positive confessors of our day very uncomfortable, because they do not reflect that line of thought.

Something good from God's point of view might be a desperate illness which suddenly puts eternity's values into perspective. Or something good from God's point of view might be a crippling financial reverse which suddenly points out the deceptive transience of material things. Just when we think we can depend on material things, a sudden reversal may reveal the true nature of this temporal world system. They are so soon gone. The Bible warns us to watch out for stormy weather, no matter how spiritual we are. Read about the prophets, about the disciples, about anyone in the Bible, and find they suffered affliction, opposition, and persecution. They suffered physically and emotionally. They suffered depression and discouragement. They are folks just like us and God used them, and God can work in our lives just as He worked in their lives.

The psalmist asks God to look at his affliction and deliver him because he doesn't forget His law. He was doing what God expected him to do. He was obedient and kept the law at the forefront and yet was still afflicted. He gives a comforting appraisal that not all suffering is punitive. It can be an instrument to develop character and conviction God can use in our lives.

Verse 154 speaks of an advocate. "Plead my cause" is a legal description. He wishes for someone to defend him, to be his advocate. We have God's Word that we do have an advocate. "My little children, these things write I unto you, that ye sin not. And if any man sin, we have an advocate with the Father, Jesus Christ the righteous" (1 John 2:1). The psalmist is ahead of his time here, but he asks the Lord to be his advocate. The truth is, as Christians, we have two advocates. We have the Lord Jesus Christ, and we have the Holy Spirit. "And he that searcheth the hearts knoweth what is the mind of the Spirit, because he maketh intercession for the saints according to the will of God" (Rom. 8:27).

This persistent affliction has driven the psalmist further toward God in his heart and mind. He apprises himself of the fact that suffering is an instrument in the hand of God and asks God to be his advocate.

In assessing the situation around him, he sings, "Salvation is far from the wicked: for they seek not thy statutes. Great are thy tender mercies, O Lord: quicken me according to thy judgments" (vv. 155-156). *First, he speaks of the pursuits of the wicked.* What do the wicked seek? They don't seek the statutes of God, and because their pursuit is away from God, the salvation of God is far from them. This verse is a solemn word to unsaved people. It makes it plain that salvation is far from the wicked. There are times when salvation is near and when the Holy Spirit is real. There are times when our consciences and hearts are tender. The Holy Spirit warns us not to miss such moments.

The psalmist explains why salvation is far away from many human beings, why they continue on in their sins. ". . . For they seek not thy statutes" (v. 155b). There are none so blind as those who will not see, and there are none so lost as those who will not seek. It is bad enough if the wicked are far from salvation, but it is worse when salvation is far from the wicked, when God pulls His salvation away. ". . . Thy seek not thy statutes." That is the reason. The result is: "Salvation is far from the wicked."

"Great are thy tender mercies, O Lord: quicken me according to thy judgments" (v. 155). *The psalmist now speaks of His provision.* It is intriguing to notice the great balance in God's dealing with us. He speaks first of "thy mercies" and then of "thy judgments." God deals with us with balance. First, there is sunshine;

then there is shadow—never too much of either one. It is not all mercy. If God gave us a blanket pardon and absolved us from all the guilt and consequences of sin, then we would never grow or mature. Often God lets the scars remain to remind us of the serious consequences of our sin. Often He allows us to remember the pain so we will not make the same mistake twice. It is not all mercy, nor is it all judgment. If it were all judgment, there would be a stern application of the letter of the law. If that were the case, we would all be hopelessly, desperately lost. We don't want justice. We want mercy. There is a balance between mercy and judgment. We are not free to do as we please, and it is not hopelessly a case of judgment. It is a mixture of the two.

The word "great" in the original language is interpreted "many." "Many" are thy tender mercies. Many ways God has revealed His mercy to us. Many ways has He moved in love to minister to us. He has drawn us to His heart in many ways. "Many" and "great" are the mercies of God. They are exceedingly rich, whether they be many, great, or both. The mercies of God toward us are overwhelming.

In the next two verses, he turns again to his pernicious attackers. They have made his situation one of gravity. "Many are my persecutors and mine enemies; yet do I not decline from thy testimonies" (v. 157). We have all ridden a bicycle downhill. It is easy to go downhill, but it is tough to ride a bicycle uphill. Being a believer is not a joy ride. Some people give the impression that being a believer is like riding a bicycle downhill. The psalmist didn't find it that way. In fact, everywhere he looked there were unfriendly faces and people who opposed him. He was tempted to give up, but he didn't. "Yet I do not decline from thy testimonies."

There are two major themes in Ephesians. There Paul talks about our *blessings* and our *battles*. Both of them are found in the "heavenlies." Our wealth is in the heavenlies, but so is our warfare. It is not a picnic to follow the Lord. There is opposition from those who will try to lure us from fellowship with the Lord.

In verse 158 we find "grief." "I beheld the transgressors, and was grieved; because they kept not thy word." The word "trans-gressors" literally means "traitors," "treacherous ones." The psalmist was surrounded by traitors, men with no principle and devoid of honor. But notice his attitude. He saw them and was "grieved." Grief is a word of love. We do not grieve about some-one unless we care about them or love them. We grieve when someone we love turns against us, when they betray us or let us down. That is a desperate grief.

The psalmist is not writing about unnamed enemies who just happen not to like what he stands for. He is surrounded by people he has loved, and they have betrayed him. He is grieved over them. Notice that he was grieved because they "kept not thy word." He was not so grieved simply because they opposed him or because they had betrayed him. He was grieved because they had not kept God's laws, because they had violated and rebelled against God's revelation. They were guilty of treason against God. That is what broke his heart. He felt no temptation to join them. He was bro-kenhearted because of their departure from the Word of God.

The closer we get to God and the more genuinely we endeavor to keep His Word, the commands of God, the more it grieves us when others don't. It hurts us. We are not angry, but we are genu-inely hurt and grieved when people we love turn their backs on God and walk away. The closer we come to God, the more we recoil from those whose lives and thoughts are against God. The severest tragedy in America is that we have become accustomed to the rebellion of our society against God and are no longer of-fended by it.

The last two verses speak of the proper attitude to have. And it reveals thought that is even more pertinent to us. "Consider how I love thy precepts: quicken me, O Lord, according to thy loving-kindness" (v. 159). The word "quicken" that appears three times in this section is used nine times in all of Psalm 119. It means "to give life" or "to restore life." This presents a very crucial turn in this psalm. It is impossible to be attached to the Word of God without knowing its quickening power, but it is entirely possible to be devoted to the Word of God and not be revived or spiritually tuned in to God. Consider "how I love thy precepts." There is nothing wrong with his devotion to the Bible. We are in a day among evangelicals where it is popular to thump the Bible, talk about how much we believe it, and how much we love it. I am for that. That is right, but we can thump the Bible and talk about believing it and still not be spiritual. Just because we use all the right clichés and all the correct words to describe the Bible does not mean we are walking with God. In fact, in the name of God and from people who profess to love the Word of God, has issued more venom and hatred in our day than perhaps in many years.

Now read me clearly. *We should not be less devoted to the Word of God.* We should be fully devoted to it, but that devotion is no guarantee of spirituality. The Bible itself warns that the letter of the law kills. If we apply the teachings of the Word of God without the Spirit of God or the love of God quickening our spirit, we will be led quickly, if not to practical heresy, to principle heresy. There was nothing wrong with his devotion to the Word of God, but that is not the same as devotion to the Lord. We love the Bible, but we do not worship the Bible. It is not our idol. We do not have biblical idolatry. The Bible doesn't save us. It only points us to the Savior. Jesus is the one who saves. The purpose of the Bible is to point us to the incarnate Word, Jesus Christ, and to teach us the truth about how to be saved, but the Bible does not save us. We are to be devoted to and love the Word of God but understand that we are to reach beyond it to the Christ and to the salvation it reveals. The Bible is indispensable, but it is not *the* way. Jesus is *The Way*.

The psalmist, interestingly enough, thought he needed revival in spite of the fact that he loved the Bible. We must go beyond the mechanical observance and faithfulness to the Word and on to a living relationship with the Christ this Word tells us about. We can quote Scripture all day long and not be spiritual. The dagger that hurts the worst proceeds from the one who says, "Brother, I love you, but, . . ."

The psalmist says, "Lord, consider how I love Thy statutes. I am willing for you to examine Me." There was nothing wrong with his devotion, but he prayed, "Lord, I need revival. Quicken me. I need being brought to life." We ought to have such a deep enthusiasm for what God is doing, such an eager anticipation that the air is filled with electricity. His devotion was OK, but he still needed revival.

And he asked to be quickened according to God's grace, according to His "lovingkindness." He was well aware his devotion to the Word of God could never take the place of a quickened relationship with God Himself.

He concludes with a strong declaration. "Thy word is true from the beginning; and every one of thy righteous judgments endureth for ever" (v. 160). The Word of God points us to Christ. By the Word we are saved because the Word reveals to us the way to God, to salvation. The Word does not save us, but it does give us assurance. God speaks to us through His Word. But if we are to have assurance from the Word of God, we must assert with the psalmist, "Thy word is true from the beginning." It is all true. If we do not affirm and believe it is true, it is of no value in our coming to conclusions or giving us assurance—or anything else. The psalmist's statement is, "Thy Word is nothing but truth."

Here is the psalmist, experiencing affliction and opposition and grieved at the unbelief of people he loved. He followed the most sensible course of action: he retreated into the one source of certainty in this universe, the Word of God. He came back to the Word of God and built his case. He realized even with that, he needed a fresh touch from God upon his life.

We can be mechanically orthodox, but that does not please God. It is good to be correct and proper, but we must have the touch of God that gives us life and a spirit of anticipation and enthusiasm. Our devotion is commendable, but we still must be quickened by the Spirit of God.

21

Peace in the Midst of the Storm

Psalm 119:161-168

I. **AWESOME:** v. 161

1. Persecution: v. 161*a*
2. Power: v. 161*b*

II. **ABHORRENCE:** vv. 162-164

1. Discovered: v. 162
2. Despised: v. 163
3. Delighted: v. 164

III. **APPROVAL:** v. 165

1. Serenity: v. 165*a*
2. Stability: v. 165*b*

IV. **ACKNOWLEDGMENT:** vv. 166-168

1. Expectation: v. 166
2. Excitement: v. 167
3. Exposed: v. 168

The psalmist has been under constant pressure, been discouraged, been depressed, and been harassed. He calls these tensions persecution and affliction. He likes to repeat those two words. It seems as if every stanza mentions the opposition, the pressures, the intimidation he faces. Yet, through it all he has maintained a faith in God and a commitment to the Word of God. His heart keeps turning back to God's Word. He meditates on it, studies it, and obeys it. He keeps its commandments. Over and over again he magnifies the place of God's Word in his life.

As we reach this next-to-last section, we discover the same situation. "Princes have persecuted me without a cause: but my heart standeth in awe of thy word" (v. 161). There is good news and bad news in this verse. *The bad news is that he is still under persecution.* The good news is: It is the last time he mentions it! He is putting it behind him. He refers to the opposition, the persecution, and the fact that he is being persecuted by important people who are in positions of authority. Princes are persecuting him. But now he permanently rises above the persecution and the opposition. He puts it behind him, and it ceases to haunt him anymore. It is now time for him to possess full victory over all of the opposition he has experienced. God's Word has finally done its work.

Let me pause to make this point: We need to give God time to work. In some matters, God is not in nearly as big of a hurry as we are. In others, He is in a bigger hurry than we are. Obviously, He is in a bigger hurry to win the lost than we are. Yet, God is also very deliberate as He develops character in us. If we trek carefully through this 119th Psalm, we see a man's pilgrimage through discouragement, through depression, through persecution, through intimidation, through affliction, through every conceivable kind of difficulty.

Yet, through it all we see him still reading his Bible, still memorizing Scripture, still praising God, still meditating on it. It seems as though it worked for a minute—then he would be back in his depression again. He is almost like a Ping Pong ball bouncing off the wall, going back and forth from one place to another. We might have the tendency to comment, "It's not working for him. He obeys and trusts God. He's true to God. It's not getting the job done." We often hear people claim, "I've tried Christianity, and it didn't work. I've tried faith, and it didn't work." The kind of commitment required for victory is a faith that says, "I believe, and I trust God." Period. No strings. No conditions on God before we believe. We don't require Him to clear all our doubts or remove all our obstacles, soften our afflictions before we believe. So much of the time, we want to bargain with God. "I will believe if . . ." or "I believe because . . ." The walk of faith, the sign of maturity is when a persons says, "I trust You, God."

It is not hard to have faith when we feel we have manipulated God into giving us what we want. It is not hard to have faith when we get the job we have waited for after we have been employed. It is hard to have faith when we stay unemployed. It is difficult to have faith when our afflictions remain. It is not easy to have faith when our disease kills us. What we recognize in this psalm is an invaluable pattern for the Christian. The entire psalm has the psalmist crying about his afflictions and persecutions. But he keeps saying, "Yet I have kept Thy word. I have not turned away from Your statutes. I have obeyed Your commandments. My delight is in Your law." He expressed an unconditional kind of commitment.

If we want a genie-type religion where we rub the lamp and get anything we want, the Bible is not for us. If we want a religion where we manipulate God and get anything we want, then Christianity is not the one. "New Age" philosophy is that kind of religion, not Christianity. Christian faith insists, "God is faithful, even when it seems to human logic that He isn't. God is true, even when I cannot understand it." The psalmist working through his problems and his difficulties never came to understand fully what he was facing—the inconsistencies of his moods and why he couldn't be freed from his problems. But what he kept hanging onto was his trust in God.

"Princes have persecuted me without a cause: but my heart standeth in awe of thy word" (v. 161). Here is a man being oppressed, afflicted, and persecuted by princes, governors, and kings. But he refuses to be intimidated. He is awestruck all right but not by the princes that persecute him. *He is overwhelmed by the power of God's Word.* The young people today like the word "awesome." It is an apropos word. *The psalmist says God's Word*

is awesome, not the princes that persecuted him. He stood in awe
of it. How refreshing. We are in a day when we want God to answer to our logic, to succumb to our judgments. If God doesn't
explain it to us, we reject it. That is the essence of liberal theology.
It is a real battle in the religious world today, a tragic struggle
between God and reason, between the infinite and the rational.
Man stands and tells God what he wants. If anyone had a right to
do that, the psalmist did. He did not have many bright days, but
his reaction was awe concerning God's Word.

Most people are in awe of the President of the United States or a
king of another country. It is an intimidating experience. But the
psalmist was in awe of the Word of God. Questions being raised
about the veracity and consistency of the Word of God are not
new. Every single question that modern theology has brought to
bear on the Scripture was settled within the first couple of centuries after the birth of Christ. There is nothing new. It is just that
man's skepticism is bolder. Man's courage is misplaced. The
psalmist chose not to be intimidated by the big shots, but rather he
chose to be in awe of the Word of God.

No wonder he finally comes through to victory. It is one thing to
gain peace after the war is over, but it is quite another to obtain
peace in the midst of the storm. What we need is not for God to
relieve the pressure, so we can feel better, but to find peace in the
midst of the pressure. If we find peace during the storm, then we
will have peace regardless. If our peace demands that the pressure
be removed, then as soon as the pressure is back, we lose our
peace. The psalmist is describing an awesome sense of reverence
and respect for the Word of God, and his obedience to the Word of
God has given him peace in the midst of the storm.

"I rejoice at thy word, as one that findeth great spoil" (v. 162).
There have been some real treasures discovered in our time. We
have uncovered the Titanic. A Spanish galleon that was full of gold
was discovered. The psalmist became so excited at God's Word,
he was like someone who had found a great treasure just like tons
of gold bullion from a Spanish galleon. He is not intimidated by

those who would attack him; *he is excited about what he has discovered in the Word of God*. It is as though, if he had his choice of the things of the world and the things of the Word of God, he chose the Word. We are often looking for a rational reason to do what we are doing. And we are constantly trying to figure out a different way other than the way God said to do it. The psalmist chose to do it God's way, whether or not he understood it. We want to react our way, but then we also want God's blessings and God's strength. We want to spend our time reading magazines or newspapers, occasionally reading the Word of God, and then want God to bless us. The psalmist found that the greatest treasure of his life was the Word of God.

When we love something or someone intensely, we are prone to extremes. *If we love to extremes, we are also likely to despise dramatically*. That happened in the case of the psalmist. "I hate and abhor lying: but thy law do I love" (v. 163). There are two contrasts in this verse. "I hate . . . I love" is one contrast. "Lying . . . the law" is another. He contrasts hate and loving and lying and the law.

The word "lying" is his reference to false religious doctrine, false religious hope. It hints at the false religions of his day. God's Word is truth absolutely. Anything else is false. We either have truth or falsehood. There is no such thing as a little bit of truth or a little bit of falsehood. If it is not true, it is false. A dreadful tragedy today is: There is so much that sounds right, so many ideas that may sound like the real thing. So much that sounds good goes under the guise of Christianity. The most dangerous heresy is the one that sounds the most like the truth. We try to use milder tones, but God says anything that is not truth is lying, falsehood.

It is not that we are to hate, nor did the psalmist, hate the people. Many false teachers believe what they teach. We hate the falsehood. Religious falsehood is the most dangerous falsehood of all because it not only deceives, it also damns and destroys. That is why the psalmist employs such strong language.

"Seven times a day do I praise thee because of thy righteous judgments" (v. 164). *He was delighted not only in the morning, at noon, or at night.* The psalmist would greet his waking moments with a word of praise. Seven times a day could actually stand for continual praise since seven is the Hebrew number of perfection.

That would be a good example for all of us to follow, not merely pausing seven times a day to pray to ask God for gifts, for guidance, or for grace, but simply to praise Him, to thank Him for being the kind of God He is—loving and kind, omniscient, omnipotent, omnipresent, faithful, and true.

Seven merely signifies a comparatively large number as Psalms 12:7 would also seem to indicate. The perfect tense of the verbs used here and repeatedly throughout the rest of the section expresses that which is habitual.

"Great peace have they which love thy law: and nothing shall offend them" (v. 165). *This speaks of approval.* There are two benefits, two results of the kind of attitude the psalmist has displayed. We make our commitment to God, period. With no strings attached, when we trust God and love His Word, two things will happen. *First, we will have great peace—serenity.* In Hebrew, it simply means "a rich measure of well-being that lacks nothing." One of the benefits for the person who walks with God and loves, obeys, meditates on, and yields his life to the Word of God is great peace. He needs nothing else.

The second benefit is stability. ". . . Nothing shall offend them." This phrase can be translated "nothing shall make them stumble." They have such deep peace, they lack nothing, and they will not fall. Nothing that happens to them can cause them to fall. No words can make them fall. No one can intimidate them into falling. Regardless of the temptations put before them, they cannot be pressured into denying God.

The psalmist concludes this section with a tremendous acknowledgment. "Lord, I have hoped for thy salvation and done thy commandments" (v. 166). Here is the sincere longing of a godly man. His sincerity and his longing are always marked by faithfulness in observing the Lord's commandments. He acknowledged that he had focused his hope on God's salvation. If this had been written in the New Testament, he would have been talking about the Lord's return. In the meantime, he was obedient. That is sound counsel. *His expectation is centered on the salvation of God, and he is faithfully observing the Lord's commandments.*

And he is excited about it. "My soul hath kept thy testimonies; and I love them exceedingly" (v. 167). "Exceedingly" is a superlative. It is not difficult to do something we love to do anyway. The psalmist loves God's Word so completely, he also loves doing what God tells him to do. What excitement he had! He has an enthusiastic and energetic love for God, so it is natural for him to be obedient.

"I have kept thy precepts and thy testimonies: for all my ways are before thee" (v. 168). To this point, it would be easy to think the psalmist is bragging on himself. He almost sounds a little arrogant, until we reach the last phrase: "For all my ways are before thee." He is saying, "I have delighted in your Word. Lord, you know that is true because you know my heart. I have kept your commandments, and you know that is true because you have observed all I have done. Lord, your praise has continually been upon my lips. Lord, you know that is true because you are mindful of every word I have spoken. Lord, my thoughts have been turned toward you, and you know that is true because you understand all the imaginations of my heart. My devotion and my affection have been toward you, and you know that is true because you see the nature of the heart. You not only know what I do but why I do it. All my ways are before you." *He is exposed.*

His first motive for keeping the Word of the Lord is from his heart. That is his love. His second motive is from his mind. That means it is not unreasonable at all. In fact, it makes perfect sense. "If God knows everything I do, then I had better be right. If God knows everything I think, then I had better think the right things." His heart loves doing what God instructs him to do, and his mind tells him that is the best thing to do because God knows everything about his heart and his mind. He lays it all before God. The psalmist is not bragging but humbly says, "The best I know I have honored God and kept His commandments. All my ways are before Him."

When we find ourselves in a storm, we need, not for the storm to be over, but for peace to come in the midst of the storm. If the storm is over before we receive peace, it will not be long before we are back in another storm, and will not know how to handle it, either. God wants to give peace regardless of what we are facing. He loves us. He doesn't laugh at our pressure—for he wants us to have peace. The writer of Hebrews put it this way, "For we have not an high priest which cannot be touched with the feeling of our infirmities" (4:15a). That means our High Priest, the Lord Jesus Christ, is touched with everything that touches us. If we hurt, He hurts. If we are under pressure, He is under pressure with us. He is there. What we need to discover is peace in the midst of the storm. Then, when the storm comes and goes, the peace will remain.

The psalmist discovered this settling truth by his faithfulness, his unswerving loyalty to the Word of God and his continual praise of God. We can have peace in the middle of the storm, "the peace of God, which passeth all understanding" (Phil. 4:7a). That kind of peace does not arise casually but from the life-style demonstrated by the psalmist. He kept loving God, praising God, and reading, meditating on, and obeying His Word . . . and God gave him peace.

22

The Key to Approaching God

Psalm 119:169-176

I. **DESIRE:** vv. 169-170

II. **DECLARATION:** vv. 171-173

III. **DELIGHT:** vv. 174-175

IV. **DISCLOSURE:** v. 176

In this finale of the psalmist's symphony about the Word of God, we sense his utter dependence on God. The section is a request, a petition, stressing his dependence. If we are going to benefit the most from life, it is important for us to understand our dependence on God. The psalmist prays in humility, recognizing his utter need of God's deliverance.

This concluding section reveals several amazing surprises for our human logic. We will see the seeming contradiction to the way human beings think as we go through this section and particularly as we get to the end.

Verses 169 and 170 give us the first key to approaching God. "Let my cry come near before thee, O Lord: give me understanding according to thy word. Let my supplication come before thee: deliver me according to thy word." The psalmist is asking for understanding, as he has done several times before. *This is his desire*. He has knowledge, and he can recite Scripture. He has even committed it to memory and has a vast amount of information about Scripture. There is a difference between knowledge and understanding. We may be well-versed in knowledge, in facts, but woefully lacking in understanding. Knowledge may simply be the accumulation of facts, but understanding is the ability to comprehend facts and take that comprehension and apply it to various experiences and circumstances.

The psalmist's desire is not just what he wants to know but why he knows it. He realizes that any understanding has to come from the Word of God. ". . . According to thy word." He is deeply cognizant of the fact that the only place to find real answers for the perplexing problems of life is the Word of God. Human logic cannot help us; human understanding cannot give us answers when we are dealing with ultimate issues like death, eternity, tragedy, and suffering. The answers to the significant issues of life are in the Word of God.

The word "deliver" in verse 170 comes from a root that means "to rescue" or "to snatch away from the hands of an enemy." The psalmist has circumstances from which he wants to be rescued, and he wants to understand why God is dealing with him as He is. He has prayed and nothing has happened. He still finds his circumstances the same, and he wants to understand why. All of us have wondered why things happen as they do, and we have been perplexed by the strange twists and turns in the road of life. It has puzzled us how and why things occur, and the psalmist is going through this same questioning. He not only wants to be delivered from his difficulties but also from his doubts. He not only wants to know what has happened but why. *That is his desire here.*

Beginning at verse 171 is a second key. *It is found in a declaration:* "My lips shall utter praise, when thou hast taught me thy statutes. My tongue shall speak of thy word: for all thy commandments are righteousness. Let thine hand help me; for I have chosen thy precepts" (vv. 171-173). He has learned God's statutes from others. That is where most of us begin—by learning the Word of God from other people. That is one of the major tasks of

the church. As we grow up we learn words that we may not understand, but that is like putting money in the bank. We never know
when we might need to draw it out. The time will come when God
draws it out and uses in our lives. The psalmist has learned the
statutes of the Lord.

The word "utter" literally means "to bubble over," "to pour
forth." So it speaks of the lips of the psalmist bubbling over with
praise for God. He cannot contain it. It reminds me of an experience that young people today are deprived of. When we were
young, soda pops came in bottles. The fun came in putting one in
the freezer and leaving it just long enough so when it was opened,
it froze. The drink became so explosive in the bottle that when the
cap was opened even a little bit, it would spew out. That is the
meaning of this word "utter." The psalmist's lips were bursting
forth with praise for God. It ought to be true in our lives. If we
learn God's statutes and apply them to our lives, our lips will bubble over with the praise of the Lord.

It is noteworthy that after his lips bubble over with praise, he
sings of his tongue speaking the Word of God. Most of our tongues
speak our own words. They are often deceptive, defiant words.
Our lips often speak disrespectful, derisive, damaging words.
Sadly, that is our kind of language. James observed:

> If any man offend not in word, the same is a perfect man,
> and able also to bridle the whole body. Behold, we put bits in
> the horses' mouths, that they may obey us; and we turn about
> their whole body. Behold also the ships, which though they
> be so great, and are driven of fierce winds, yet are they
> turned about with a very small helm, whithersoever the gov-
> ernor listeth. Even so the tongue is a little member, and
> boasteth great things. Behold, how great a matter a little fire
> kindleth! (3:2-5).

If we could do away with the damaging, divisive words we
speak to each other, many of today's problems would be elimi-
nated, especially in the Christian world.

The psalmist declares that his tongue will speak God's Word. If we could only harness our tongues like that! How will our tongues speak the Word of God? There are two ways. We can read out loud, or we can memorize it and recite it. One of the best means of praising God is to quote Scripture. Try reading the Psalms out loud to God. It becomes a thrilling exercise in praise. It is supernatural when our tongues speak God's words. Our words are so inadequate and often so evil and insensitive. The psalmist's testimony, in choosing God's precepts, was a declaration.

The word "chosen" pictures a priceless treasure he has selected. He has chosen and committed himself to the Word of God, and he thus appeals directly to God. "Let *thine* hand help me" (v. 173, italics mine). He goes directly to the throne because God's hand is the only hand that can help him. We often appeal to others for assistance, but the psalmist asked for God's helping hand. His declaration is that his lips will utter God's praise and his tongue will speak the Word, for he had deliberately chosen God's precepts.

"I have longed for thy salvation, O Lord; and thy law is my delight. Let my soul live, and it shall praise thee: and let thy judgments help me" (vv. 175-176). *He has a great delight in Scripture.* His desire to be delivered from trouble had not dimmed his delight in the Word of God. Many times when people have gone through protracted periods of difficulty, when they find ourselves in stressful and distressing circumstances, caught in a vice grip of doubt, they take out their frustrations on God. Such an attitude is reprehensible, but it seems to be common. People often complain, when caught in a particular kind of tragedy, "If that is the kind of God He is, then I don't want to have anything to do with Him."

Many have abandoned the Word of God altogether under the pressure of disappointment and discouragement—but not the psalmist. In spite of everything, he longed for God's salvation. He delighted in the law. He had nowhere else to go, and neither do we. If one abandons the Bible, he abandons hope. There is no salvation in scientific theories of mankind; no relief in the social philosophies of our age; no redemption in the religious ideologies of this world.

God has shut us up to His Word, and that is the end of it. There is no place else to go. This was vividly demonstrated when Jesus asked the disciples what had happened to all the vast throngs of people who had followed him. When Simon Peter told Him they had left, Jesus inquired, "Will ye also go away?" Peter answered, "Lord, to whom shall we go? thou hast the words of eternal life" (John 6:67-68). There is no place else to go. There is no other way. The psalmist, in spite of his disappointments, found his delight in the law of God. Nothing had worked out as he had hoped, but he continued to trust God and long for His presence. If we want to have victory, delighting in the law of God must be a reality in our lives.

Verse 175 is actually a prayer with three aspects to it. First, "Let my soul live." He is aware of deadness, dryness within. Over and over he has expressed his delight and dependence on the Word of God, yet his soul is dry. We can identify with him. We can often be so committed to studying the Word of God, spending many hours reading and memorizing it, and yet our souls can still be dry. The psalmist is asking for excitement and enthusiasm, the wonder that once was there. The tragedy is when we become content with mere knowledge about the Word of God, and we lose that sensitivity, that aliveness, about the Word of God.

The second aspect of the prayer is a promise to praise God with the new life—life flowing in, love flowing out, a living soul expressing itself in a song of praise. Praise is the heartbeat of the soul, a reality of life and the natural response of life. Then he wants God's Word to help him in expressing that new life within. This is his prayer.

Verse 176 is the surprise. After 175 verses of deep commitment to, praise for, delight in, and expressions about the Word of God, this verse looks out of place. "I have gone astray like a lost sheep; seek thy servant; for I do not forget thy commandments" (v. 176).

We would think by now the psalmist would be a super saint. He certainly would be far down the road to maturity. No, far from it! We discover that the further down the road of faith we go, and the longer we walk with the Lord, the more we realize how firmly entrenched evil can be in our lives. We have all wondered why when God seems to move powerfully in a church, the first ones to walk down the aisle with tears, renewing their commitment to God, are those we thought were the most spiritual saints in the church. The reason is: the closer we come to God, the more aware we are of our sinfulness. The nearer sinful man gets to Holy God, the greater the contrast. If we do not feel a sensitivity to sin, that is not a mark of spirituality—it is a mark of carnality. The closer we approach God, the more we will be aware of our limitations, our selfishness, arrogance, and pride. The closer we get to Him and experience His holiness and sense His presence, the more we realize how far short we fall.

Here at the very end of Psalm 119 is a startling, surprising disclosure. First, we see the psalmist straying like a lost sheep. It is an honest confession. It is the nature of sheep to stray. Sheep do not get together and stray. They do that naturally. They do not have to be exceedingly wicked to stray. It is not malicious—just by their nature they stray. A sheep has to be led. Leave it alone, and it will stray. That is basic to being a sheep. In the same sense, it is human nature for us to stray. "All we like sheep have gone astray; we have turned every one to his own way . . ." (Isa. 53:6a). We allow the crowding concerns of everyday life to loom too large in our lives. We become too involved in the urgent and miss the important. Have you discovered that urgent matters are seldom important and important matters are seldom urgent? Here is an emergency, and it consumes us. Too often the concerns God told us not to be concerned about loom too large in our lives, and we do "what comes naturally." We stray, and we become cold toward God.

That disclosure is so true to life. Many times we are so busy serving God and doing what God has asked us to do, and yet our hearts have waxed cold toward God. Because we can recite Scripture, we love the Word, and want to obey it, we interpret our lack of conviction as maturity when it is really a blatant testimony of going astray. The closer we get to God, the more we understand we need to commit our lives to walk closer to Him.

Here a psalmist, spiritual enough to write Psalm 119 and sensitive enough to follow the Holy Spirit's guidance in doing it, comes to the end and confesses, "I have gone astray like a lost sheep." Then we see him praying. "Seek thy servant, come find me." A sheep won't come back by itself; it has to be found. So the psalmist's prayer is for God to come after him.

Then he makes a strange statement. ". . . For I do not forget thy commandments." It means one of two things. Either it is an inducement or an indictment. If it is an inducement, he is saying to God. "I have gone astray like a lost sheep but, God, come get me, because I do not forget your commandments." It is an inducement for God to pursue him. Does God need an inducement to seek His sheep? Does it impress God enough that the psalmist hasn't forgotten His commandments to the extent that God is induced to seek him? It may be an inducement. It may be the psalmist's reasoning. Perhaps he speaks about his personal desire.

But maybe it is an indictment. To have God's Word stored in our hearts, to be able to quote Scripture, to be able to testify, "I have obeyed the laws and commands of God," and still go astray, is serious business. It is one case for a lost sinner, who has no understanding of the Word of God, to go astray. But it is quite another for an intelligent, knowledgeable believer, with all of the inducements of the Word of God and the understanding that accompanies it, still to go astray. How serious it is for someone to go astray, yet quoting Scripture and understanding much of God's Word.

And thus he closes the longest chapter in God's Word. It is over. "I have gone astray; seek me; I do not forget thy commandments." He ends the psalm still reaching out for God. The truth is we may lose sight of God and go astray like a dumb sheep, but God never loses sight of us. He still seeks us. When our hearts are open, we will be found of Him and He of us. This is a magnificent conclusion to this psalm.

We are living in a day when Bible knowledge is magnified. More than knowledge, we must have understanding. Today, many of us Christians possess a vast store of biblical truth, but we also have a desperate need: hearts that are sensitive toward God and lives that are in harmony with Him. We do not need to stray quoting Scripture. We need God to infuse life, enthusiasm, and liberty in our hearts.